The Center for South and Southeast Asia Studies of the University of California is the unifying organization for faculty members and students interested in South and Southeast Asia Studies, bringing together scholars from numerous disciplines. The Center's major aims are the development and support of research and language study. As part of this program the Center sponsors a publication series of books concerned with South and Southeast Asia. Manuscripts are considered from all campuses of the University of California as well as from any other individuals and institutions doing research in these areas.

PUBLICATIONS OF THE CENTER FOR SOUTH AND SOUTHEAST ASIA STUDIES:

Angela S. Burger
Opposition in a Dominant-Party System: A Study of the Jan Sangh, the Praja Socialist Party, and the Socialist Party in Uttar Pradesh, India (1969)

Robert L. Hardgrave, Jr.
Nadars of Tamilnad: The Political Culture of a Community in Change (1969)

Eugene F. Irschick
Politics and Social Conflict in South India: The Non-Brahman Movement and Tamil Separatism, 1916–1929 (1969)

Briton Martin, Jr.
New India, 1885: British Official Policy and the Emergence of the Indian National Congress (1969)

James T. Siegel
The Rope of God (1969)

Jyotirindra Das Gupta
Language Conflict and National Development: Group Politics and National Language Policy in India (1970)

Robert N. Kearney
Trade Unions and Politics in Ceylon (1971)

David N. Lorenzen
The Kāpālikas and Kālāmukhas: Two Lost Śaivite Sects (1971)

David G. Marr
Vietnamese Anticolonialism, 1885–1925 (1971)

Elizabeth Whitcombe
Agrarian Condition in Northern India. Volume One: The United Provinces under British Rule, 1860–1900 (1971)

KIN, CLAN, RAJA, AND RULE
STATE-HINTERLAND RELATIONS IN PREINDUSTRIAL INDIA

This volume is sponsored by the
Center for South and Southeast Asia Studies,
University of California, Berkeley

Richard G. Fox

KIN
CLAN
RAJA
AND
RULE

State-Hinterland Relations
in Preindustrial India

Berkeley
Los Angeles
London

UNIVERSITY OF CALIFORNIA PRESS

1971

University of California Press
Berkeley and Los Angeles, California
University of California Press, Ltd.
London, England
Copyright © 1971, by
The Regents of the University of California
Library of Congress Catalog Card Number: 76-129614
International Standard Book Number: 0-520-01807-9

To my own kin

PREFACE

T HIS STUDY investigates the behavioral and ideological interaction between local community and national society in preindustrial northern India. The investigation of the relationship between state and hinterland, between region and locality in the Indian past will I hope contribute to a comparative political anthropology and to a deeper comprehension of the nature of the state. This study also seeks to define more adequately the special qualities of Indian civilization, at least as they are reflected in the unique, culturally defined state-hinterland relations found within traditional northern India. I therefore am addressing myself to both South Asia specialists and nonspecialists; to those with much background in anthropology and to those with little.

I have purged the text of most native revenue and political terms which do so much to discourage cross-cultural research. I have not tried to regularize the spelling of Indian terms, nor do I employ diacritical marks. Indian scholars will recognize the words in any case, and the general reader will avoid the burden of numerous italicized unpronounceables. From this desire to stress the general rather than detail the specific, I have avoided extensive citation of specific personages and recounting of events in northern India during the historical period under study. Similarly, the chapter on comparative state forms is discursive and I hope, illuminative; it is not exhaustive. My object is to see general processes in Indian state-hinterland relations and regularities in cross-cultural political organization, and I sacrifice the specifics of Indian events or the uniqueness of individual political orders to this goal. Such behavior runs the risk of satisfying no scholarly specialist, and of irritating all alike. In many ways such indignation may be justified by the factual and theoretical inadequacies of this study, of which I am well aware. Sometimes, however, distaste flows from scholarly provincialism and hairsplitting, qualities which impede academic research. Must only the Indianists know India? Must only the anthropologists know their tribes? If academic research is defined so narrowly, we would all do better to pack up and take on new challenges. I believe that anthropology and South Asian studies can say more, and I have tried to show how in this essay.

Any scholar interested in using historical materials to comprehend Indian society and culture owes a great debt to the many British revenue officers who commonly were anthropologists in colonial clothing. I also gratefully acknowledge the work of the contemporary historians and anthropologists cited in the text below. I owe an especially great debt to Professor Bernard Cohn. Frequently in the following pages, my reliance on Professor Cohn's factual materials is apparent. But also in a personal sense his work convinced me that studies of past tenurial and political orders are a legitimate enterprise in the anthropology of South Asia. I also wish to acknowledge the early training in political anthropology which I received from Professor Morton H. Fried. His interests and point of view in the cross-cultural study of political organization have become my own to a large extent. I am indebted to Professor Thomas Metcalf for introducing me in depth to the revenue literature on northern India during a 1962 seminar at the University of California, Berkeley. I hope in balance that this essay will not prove a discredit to my scholarly background.

The research for the following presentation was mainly carried out from July to September, 1968 at the India Office Library of the Commonwealth Relations Office in London, England. I wish to thank the Committee on International Studies of Duke University for a summer grant which permitted the research. Preparation of the maps and typing of the manuscript were generously provided by a grant from the Program on Comparative Studies in Southern Asia, Duke University. The maps were drawn by J. B. Hobday. I would like to thank my colleagues, Professors Joseph Di Bona and Ainslee Embree, for their helpful comments on an earlier draft of this work.

CONTENTS

MAPS

CHARTS

"One great fact
forces itself on the attention,
namely, that for the last four hundred years
there have been two governments,
the imperial Muhammadan and
the local Hindu, of which the latter
was the most elastic,
the most intimately connected with the people . .
and it is out of the collision
between these two governments
that the present state of society
was produced."

*A Report on the Family History of
the Chief Clans of the Roy Bareilly
District* by W. C. Bennet

1

THE ETHNOGRAPHIC USES
OF THE PAST

NONLITERACY HAS been a severe handicap to many primitive peoples. It has also been a handicap to anthropology. As long as anthropologists studied such people formally lacking history, they were confined to synchronic, homeostatic profiles in the "ethnographic present"; that is, their studies had little time depth and were based on an equilibrium model in which the society was described as being in a state of balance. To be sure, many early scholars attempted reconstructions of cultural diffusion and development. Still others delved into oral history and legend. However, the basis for collection of historical data remained synchronic observation: the past was known only as an artifact of the present. Distinguished anthropologists such as Radcliffe-Brown and Boas railed against the use of such conjectural history in ethnographic research. This disparagement along with the theoretical excesses of the evolutionists and diffusionists led to declining scholarly involvement in even this form of historical investigation. Further thought on the value of history or its use within their discipline was spared anthropologists by the nonliteracy of the cultures they studied. Like the proverbial New Yorker whose mental geography recognizes little between Manhattan and California, anthropologists often could see little between the recent history of postcolonial contact with native peoples and the latters' undated or undatable oral legends of the past.

Even though anthropologists in the past decades have turned away from "reconstituted" or "remnant" primitives to the study of complex civilizations, the same historical myopia often continues. Clearly, anthropologists do not deny the lengthy and well-documented pasts of China, India, Japan, or Latin America. Yet they have generally concentrated on the intimate study of specific rural communities within such civilizations, and therefore often have not used much historical background in anthropological investigations. Commonly in such community studies we learn of the founding of the village—through both legendary tale and historical record. Then we are told of the effect on the village of social legislation like community development or family planning in the past fifty years. The intervening centuries of political, social, and ritual existence of the community are telescoped into the obscurity of being "traditional," a seemingly static limbo altered only by the arrival of "Westernization" or "modernization" in recent times. The result: a "nonliterate" community profile similar to those written about primitive peoples.

In complex societies, historical data are limited not by nonliteracy but by the method of the anthropologist. The theoretical "cover" of the community study method reduces his sensibilities of historical questions to what little can be obtained in a single village. The researcher may argue that reliable, written records on his village community are scant, or have to do with administrative and revenue procedures rather than social organization and group dynamics. Rather than confirming the anthropologist in his ahistorical approach, this absence of valuable historical materials should convince him to dispense with the community as a base for investigation.

To comprehend a complex society in its totality is to view its national-level traditions and social organization in interaction with community-level traditions and institutions.[1] The value of a research technique which does not link the local area to the larger society in terms of historical and contemporary social processes is highly questionable. Julian Steward, Eric Wolf, Robert Manners, Adrian Mayer, and F. G. Bailey [2] among others have all suggested that the community study method is irrelevant to complex societies because it describes Ramapur or San Juan or Koprivnica instead of India, Mexico, or Yugoslavia. A proliferation of individual rural profiles is of small theoretical and comparative significance for the analysis of the society as a whole. In strikingly similar fashion, although with differing terminologies and emphases, the above mentioned commentators suggest a supralocal or regional or "village-outward" viewpoint for the analysis of complex societies. What becomes significant, then, is the network of political,

    1. See Robert Redfield, "The Social Organization of Tradition," *Peasant Society: A Reader*, pp. 26–27.
    2. See Julian Steward, *Area Research: Theory and Practice;* Eric R. Wolf, "Aspects of Group Relations in a Complex Society: Mexico," *American Anthropologist*, LVIII (1956), 1068; Robert Manners, "Remittances and the Unit of Analysis in Anthropological Research," *Southwestern Journal of Anthropology*, XXI (1965), 179–195; Adrian Mayer, "The Significance of Quasi-Groups in the Study of Complex Societies," *The Social Anthropology of Complex Societies*, pp. 97–122; F. G. Bailey, *Politics and Social Change: Orissa in 1959.*

economic, and ritual ties linking the local community to the larger society; the manner in which these links are specifically defined by the social constitution of the individual society; and the way in which these ties are gradually altered by the larger society or conversely, are changed by the local community.

If anthropology in complex societies is to study the linkages between the local and larger society, then history is a necessary ingredient. No cultural anthropologist will ever see the Indian caste system or Indian patterns of consanguinity and affinity emerge from the mud huts and dirt lanes of Gopalpur or Raniganj. Nor will he understand changing rural-urban relationships by counting the number of oxcarts, buses, teahouses, and capitalist entrepreneurs which arrive in his village from the outside. Neither will he understand how the social constituents of his own village community such as kinship and caste have been generalized into an organizational framework which embraces the entire society. Participant-observation techniques alone provide neither a sufficiently macroscopic viewpoint nor the diachronic breadth necessary for such problems. Data lacking or not obtainable through participant-observation can often be found in historical and archival sources. The time depth permitted by historical information illuminates the nature of societal integration, its form and development in the past, and its resiliency into the present. Such time depth will also specify social causality more effectively than intuitive structural-functional analyses or presumed Marxist dialectics.

The importance of historical research for the comprehension of complex societies has been illustrated in some recent anthropological works. Maurice Freedman has written of Chinese specialists prevented by political hostility from doing fieldwork, who have adopted a historical perspective and probed historical sources for questions about societal development.[3] Clifford Geertz has written of the colonial and ecological development of Indonesia within a large-scale historical framework.[4] He has also indicated how a local community, the small market town of Modjokuto, has altered and adapted itself gradually to these developments.[5] G. William Skinner and Bernard Cohn have tried to delineate historically important marketing areas or levels of political integration in preindustrial China and northern India, respectively.[6] Robert and Barbara Anderson have combined history and anthropological field research in their investigation of a small community on the outskirts of Paris.[7]

Two common viewpoints unite all these contributions. Historical data are used to comprehend the succession or evolution of social forms or at least to understand social structure at a synchronic point in the traditional society; history is not used to provide a mere temporal sequence of dates, names, and places. More important, all these studies contain a wider scholarly horizon than the single-community study. Even the Andersons' study of the French community, Wissous, evolves into a historical and contemporary survey of its relations with and integration into the Parisian region. The Andersons acknowledge both the historical and the supracommunity aspects of their work when they set as their goal:

3. Maurice Freedman, "A Chinese Phase in Social Anthropology," *British Journal of Sociology*, XIV (1963), 1–19.

4. Clifford Geertz, *Agricultural Involution: The Process of Ecological Change in Indonesia.*

5. Clifford Geertz, *The Social History of an Indonesian Town.*

6. G. William Skinner, "Marketing and Social Structure in Rural China, Part I," *Journal of Asian Studies*, XXIV (1964), 3–44; Bernard Cohn, "Political Systems in Eighteenth Century India: The Benares Region," *Journal of the American Oriental Society*, LXXXII (1962), 312–320.

7. Robert and Barbara Anderson, *Bus Stop for Paris.*

to direct an inquiry relevant to both the anthropological *and* the historical interest in the impact of national events in small, especially peasant, communities. The result is a history of the social organization of a village through almost 900 years. Yet not so much the history of a single small community as the history of France from a particular point of view.[8]

Such studies thus specify economic, political, and ecological forces binding communities to the larger society over time or at a single point in the traditional past. They shed light on the characteristic sociohistorical configurations and specific institutions of societal integration in complex societies.

This study is based on the premise that historical investigations which are focused beyond the local community can illuminate many anthropological questions about social institutions and social processes in complex societies. My primary objective is to analyse the historical structure of local-level political groups and how they interacted with state governmental machinery in parts of northern India. Historical materials gathered from the revenue and ethnographic reports of nineteenth-century British civil servants will be used to answer the following questions: In what way did the local area organize its political autonomy? In what way was local political organization influenced or transformed by power or duties delegated from the central authority? How did changing balances of power between the state and locality alter the organization of political groups?

Specifically, this study discusses the historical interrelations of localized unilineal kin bodies—Rajput "clans" and their elites—with state-level administrative and revenue institutions. This analysis presupposes a supracommunity

8. *Ibid.*, p. 4.

approach. It uses historical materials to analyze important evolutionary developments rather than merely to chart temporal sequences. The relevance of this study to anthropology is two-fold. First, the analysis specifies the various sociopolitical factors of the larger society that defined the territorial dispersion, genealogical depth, internal stratification, and land tenure of such localized Rajput "clans." From this viewpoint, the local community is indeed the lower terminus of its economic, political, and ritual links to the state. Second, the analysis indicates how the organizational constituents of the Indian rural community such as caste and kinship provided political and ideological forms for the larger society. In this light the state stands defined by the many localities and communities of which it is composed and by which it is structured.

The paragraphs directly below advance some general notions about state-hinterland interaction and prepare the conceptual base for later chapters. Chapter two analyses the unilineal kin structure of various castes claiming Rajput or Kshatriya status in northern India; the chapter discusses how such kin bodies were modified by their enjoyment of delegated state authority and therefore partial, local autonomy; further, the chapter portrays the shared ideology of genealogical descent which linked corporate kin organization at the localized level with increasingly ramified groups such as the caste and subregional varna; the same chapter also describes the elite of such kin groups, both as they were defined by genealogical criteria and by the performance of state administrative duties; the nature of the North Indian state and its pertinence to local kin bodies is also discussed. The chapter thus takes a synchronic slice out of the traditional political life of northern India.

Chapter three attempts to go beyond this sociologically static description by employing a developmental cycle model of the Rajput "clan;" the chapter examines the birth, maturing process, and demise of kin groups within the political framework of the preindustrial North Indian state; it also tries to discover the causal factors underlying each developmental stage.

In chapter four, the historical materials from northern India are given a larger, comparative context by analysis of state formation and organization in societies of the ethnographic present and the archaeological past; this chapter also reviews the literature within political anthropology on the nature of the state, and evaluates the role of kinship in a centralized political system; some conclusions are drawn on the origins of state organization. Chapter four thus tries to validate the Rajput data as an exercise in comparative political anthropology.

Chapter five summarizes the discussion and helps to define the unique roles of kinship and caste in the formation of the North Indian state. The foregoing Rajput and comparative materials are used to comprehend the specific qualities of Indian civilization which entered into state-hinterland interaction. With this last chapter, the narrative stands completed: the local kin-based community in northern India appears as both a definition and a definer of the larger society.

Preindustrial agrarian states were often less than the sum of their parts.[9] During the course of any dynasty local strong men and disgruntled peasants threatened, or actually dissolved, the thin film of state hegemony which bound them to the central power. Industrial states create high levels of regional economic specialization and necessary interdependence not found in simpler technologies. Industrial states also have major communication and trans-

9. For a discussion of agrarian societies, see Gerhard Lenski, *Power and Privilege,* pp. 189–296.

portation webs which cement local areas and regions to the central economic and governmental cores. Preindustrial agrarian states, however, are characterized by economically, and therefore potentially politically, self-sufficient regions—each with its own wider cultural distinctions of kinship, language, ritual observances and beliefs, customs, and "manners." An economy based primarily on the ill-coordinated household-oriented peasant producers could easily fragment into productively autonomous regions. Owen Lattimore has talked about the lack of economic centralization in such agrarian societies.[10] Bernard Cohn and F. G. Bailey have noted the potential political fragmentation within such preindustrial states in their concepts of "little kingdoms" [11] or "blocks" [12] which remain intact once higher political authority disintegrates. Preindustrial agrarian states are further characterized by primitive transportation networks, for instance oxen used to haul grain which consume more in one hundred miles than they can draw.[13] Such technological backwardness places severe limits on economic coordination, famine control, and the leveling of regional productive differentials.

Preindustrial agrarian states must continually deal politically with the inherent insularities, self-sufficiencies, and regionalisms of their undeveloped technological and productive orders. They issue punitive threats or suppress actual revolt. They bequeath sumptuary regalia or local autonomy to their many parts—each of which seeks political independence when state force or protection is re-

10. See Owen Lattimore, "The Frontier in History," *Studies in Frontier History*, pp. 478–480.

11. Bernard Cohn, Review of "Caste and Community Structure in Five Regions of India and Pakistan," *Journal of the American Oriental Society*, LXXXII (1962), 425–430.

12. F. G. Bailey, "Closed Social Stratification in India," *Archives Europeannes de Sociologie*, IV (1963), 107.

13. Lattimore, *op. cit.*, p. 479.

moved. Often scholars view this dialogue between central authority and locality solely from the state administration downward. In this light, all political activity at local and regional levels appears disruptive. We read of rebellious vassals of the ruler, of dissident localities and anarchic regions, each scheming toward, or actively engaged in, revolt. Little is said about the political priorities at the local level, and the way in which state power disrupts or redefines community organization. For example, the great controversy over state revenue intermediaries such as talukdars and zamindars in northern India stems in part from their sharing a common definition with respect to the state but having different social origins and statuses at the local level. The emphasis of this study is the web of political alliances, revenue levies, and social conventions which bound together or set at odds a locality and the preeminent state power.

The following presentation is based primarily on historical sources of the thirteenth through nineteenth centuries collected by diligent British revenue officers and amateur ethnographers. The use of these materials has many drawbacks. Their authors were not trained anthropologists or historians; their information was often highly anecdotal or even legendary, and their historical depth was limited. These are often, nonetheless some of the first authoritative sources for this information. Little seems to have been recorded in the vernacular literature of pre-British days.[14] British interest was a result of romantic attraction to the old "noble" classes of upper India; it was also a matter of having to resolve practical questions of proprietorship and revenue engagement. Undoubtedly the

14. Habib notes that historical documents from the Mughal period contain no definition of zamindar or any description of zamindari rights. The nature of local kin ties appears to have been even more overlooked or taken for granted. See Irfan Habib, *The Agrarian System of Mughal India*, p. 138.

historical materials contained in this study could be much improved and expanded, especially by the addition of data drawn from pre-British sources. Many interpretations presented here may lack insight and prove faulty, particularly because I am not a trained historian. The historian may object to the emphasis on the delineation of general processes of political interaction and kin structure to the omission of detailed examination of specific political events between state authority and local kin groupings. The anthropologist who adopts a historical approach does not thereby become a historian. My aim is to ask anthropological questions of historical material, not to duplicate the chronologies already established by nineteenth-century British revenue officers.[15] This study is meant as a preliminary and speculative analysis. Its main purpose is to elicit further anthropological-historical research, even if that research should prove this investigation wrong or deficient.

The region referred to as northern India in the following pages approximates the present state of Uttar Pradesh and the former United Provinces of Agra and Oudh during British rule. The United Provinces (U.P.) was an artificial administrative division conceived by the British colonial government (see map 1). It contained several regions with distinctive historical and cultural backgrounds. European imperialism in the form of the British East India Company entered this part of northern India at the end of the eighteenth century when local government institutions had weakened or decayed in the aftermath of the Mughal Empire's decline. The first segment to pass into the hands of the British East India Company was the Banaras territory which was officially annexed in 1795. In 1801, the Ceded Districts were given the Company by the Navab of Oudh. The Conquered Districts passed to the British in

15. Cf. Kathleen Gough's work on the Nayar in Kathleen Gough and David Schneider, eds., *Matrilineal Kinship*.

1803 after they were won by force from various Mahratta chieftains. Throughout the early decades of the nineteenth century the Conquered and Ceded Districts were known by numerous terms, among them the North-Western Provinces and Upper India. Eventually, they and the Banaras region were incorporated into the province of Agra. The most recent part of the United Provinces to be annexed by the British was the native state of Oudh, which was ruled by navabs who had achieved regional independence

MAP 1. Uttar Pradesh

after the decline of the Mughal Empire. Oudh was annexed as British territory in 1856. After the Mutiny of 1857, the separate provinces of Agra and Oudh were joined to form the United Provinces, an administrative division whose territorial boundaries persist more or less unchanged in the modern state of Uttar Pradesh.

The historical data which follow have been drawn from all parts of present-day Uttar Pradesh, but special emphasis has been placed on eastern and central U.P. districts such as Sultanpur, Faizabad, and Pratabgarh (all formerly part of Oudh), and Jaunpur, Ballia, and Ghazipur (once part of the Banaras region). I pass now to an examination of kinship and the state within this region.

2

"CLAN," RAJA, AND STATE

THE ROLE of kinship and caste in the definition of North Indian local political groups is a major focus of this essay. Although the political dialogue between state and locality existed in all preindustrial agrarian societies, its specific manifestation in a particular culture was channeled by institutions of the larger society. The preservation of unilineal kinship and its extension, caste, has often been taken as a unique characteristic of Indian civilization. Redfield wrote of India,

The principal elements of the country-wide networks of India consist of familial and caste associations that persist through generations. These associations connect one set of villages with another or some of the families in one village with families corresponding in culture and social status in other villages. It is as if the characteristic social structure of the primitive self-contained community had been dissected out and its components spread about a wide area. . . . Rural

India is a picture of a tribal society rearranged to fit a civilization.[1]

Redfield's somewhat cryptic remark will prove highly insightful in the final analysis of North Indian state formation. Without such an analytic gloss, however, it communicates more the shock of sociological recognition of Indian caste and kinship than any didactic content. Similarly, Leach has hypothesized that

caste is indissolubly linked with a Pan-Indian civilization. Consequently I believe that those who apply the term to contexts wholly remote from the Indian world invariably go astray.[2]

Leach's comments are no less cryptic than Redfield's. A structural form such as caste, which is regarded as always congruent with a specific culture, is a structural form reduced to a mere cultural trait. In this view, caste is either present or not present; how it is present and why it is present go unanswered. To note that caste and unilineal kinship are qualities of Indian civilization says little about that civilization. A more fruitful approach is employed by Pocock in a critique of rural and urban sociologies in India.[3] Pocock recognizes some fundamental structural elements in Indian civilization, but he is not content merely to mark them off a culture trait list. Rather he compares their occurrence in different realms within the society. His distaste for separate rural and urban sociologies is based on a belief that the social institutions of the

1. Robert Redfield, *Peasant Society and Culture*, p. 34.
2. E. R. Leach, ed., *Aspects of Caste in South India, Ceylon, and Northwest Pakistan*, p. 4.
3. David F. Pocock, "Sociologies—Rural and Urban," *Contributions to Indian Sociology*, IV (1960), 63–81 *passim*.

rural area, such as caste and kinship, are also the fundamental organizational units of the urban sphere. A similar
approach can be used for the political sphere. Caste and
kinship are not monolithic traits of Indian civilization.
They are important organizational institutions which can
determine at the same time the constitution of peasant
villages and the nature of the local components of the
state. To specify the different spheres in which caste and
kinship exist within Indian civilization is to indicate why
they are congruent with that civilization.

In northern India throughout the specified time period,
caste and unilineal kinship were major determinants of the
structure of state-hinterland interaction. The unilineal kin
organization of locally dominant castes claiming "Kshatriya" or "Rajput" status performed many political and
military functions. Such castes were also state-defined institutions for revenue collection, and were often delegated
police and civil powers over a local area. These unilineal
kin bodies were usually headed by rajas or chaudharis, who
were representatives both of the state and their kin group
in the locality. Partly through the ascriptive office of lineage raja, partly through their investiture with state power,
the elites of such kin, or caste, groups often presented both
the greatest threat of local revolt and the most potent guarantee of the preservation of central authority at the local
level. ("Ascriptive" refers to social status conferred by
birth or other nonachieved criteria.) The following analysis is limited to so-called Rajput kin bodies. "Rajput" is a
status title which local groups assumed as part of their
claim to social position or higher rank on a regional level.
The title required of its claimants an ideological and a
minimal behavioral commitment to a life style defined as
Rajput. In the course of Indian history and often within
close geographical proximity to Rajput groups, other lo-

cally dominant status categories emerged such as Jats, Bhuinhars, or various Muslims. At times, such "ethnically" homogeneous groups arise from a common, tribal migration. However, they also come about through the assumption by diverse local groups of a single identity and title. The ramifications of such separate ethnic histories and status claims and the organizational consequences are too great to be discussed in this study. For this reason, Rajput kin structure and Rajput interaction with the state are the primary concern in the following pages although mention is made occasionally of adjacent and often genealogically related groups which did not claim Rajput status.

KIN AND "CLAN"

Recent work by Bernard Cohn, K. N. Singh, and M. C. Pradhan has indicated the important role played by unilineal kin groups of locally dominant Kshatriya "castes" in the low-level political organization of traditional North India. For the Banaras region, Cohn notes the prevalence of *talukas,* which consisted of a "lineage of agnatically related kin of the same *biradari* (exogamous local caste group)" with important governmental, revenue, and military functions in state operations.[4] K. N. Singh provides greater detail about the organization of these kin bodies, although he seems to disagree with Cohn about terms. Singh speaks of regionally dominant Rajput lineages providing corporate political authority throughout eastern Uttar Pradesh; their internal kinship ties create administrative and economic linkages extending from the *pargana* (administrative division equivalent to a county) through

4. Cohn, "Political Systems in Eighteenth Century India: The Benares Region," *Journal of the American Oriental Society,* LXXXII (1962), 313.

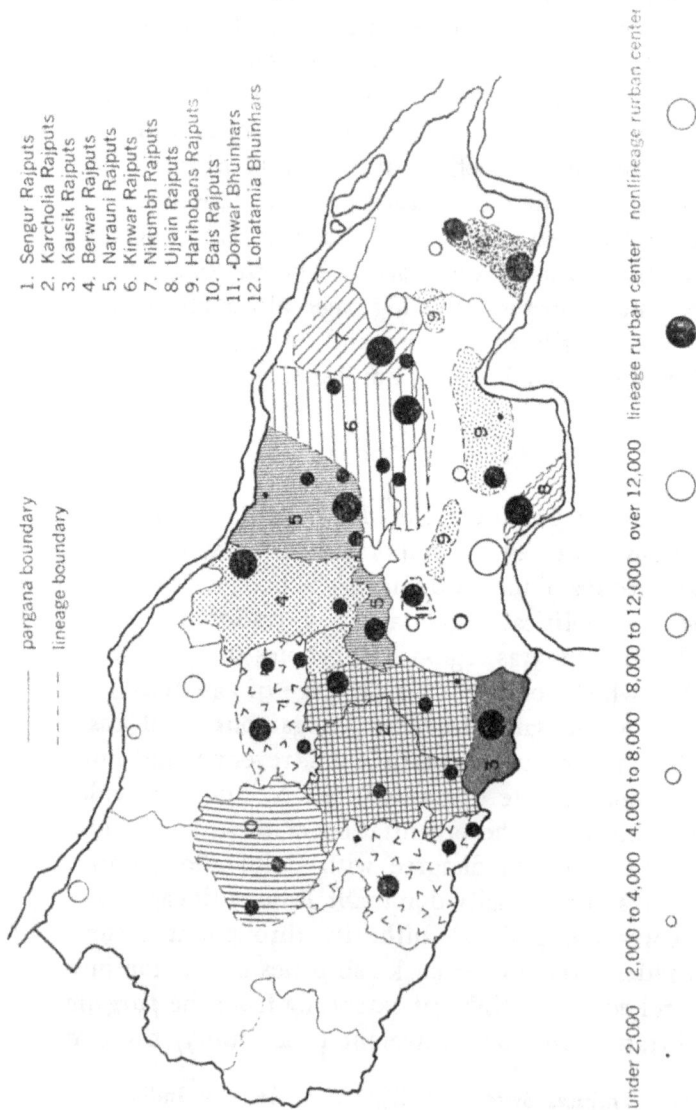

MAP 2. Lineage Distribution and Rurban Centers in Ballia District. The relationship between the boundaries of extended kin groups and administrative divisions (parganas) is indicated. Lineage rurban centers refer to the urban-like communities where the lineage elite resided. (For the location of Ballia district in Uttar Pradesh, see map 1.)

1. Sengur Rajputs
2. Karcholia Rajputs
3. Kausik Rajputs
4. Berwar Rajputs
5. Narauni Rajputs
6. Kinwar Rajputs
7. Nikumbh Rajputs
8. Ujjain Rajputs
9. Harihobans Rajputs
10. Bais Rajputs
11. Donwar Bhuinhars
12. Lohatamia Bhuinhars

——— pargana boundary
- - - - lineage boundary

under 2,000   2,000 to 4,000   4,000 to 8,000   8,000 to 12,000   over 12,000   lineage rurban center   nonlineage rurban center

the *tappa* (administrative subdivision of a pargana) and
into the *gaon* or individual village.[5] Pradhan, in his extended analysis of traditional Jat kinship, notes the existence of clan areas forming councils on a clan and subclan
("maximal lineage") basis, each under the leadership of a
chaudhari, and each interacting with the preindustrial
state in corporate fashion.[6] Map 2 indicates the distribution of extended kin groups in Ballia district, and their
relationship to the pargana administrative division.

These recent authors carry forward a sociological analysis which also captivated the early British revenue authorities, Oldham, Baden-Powell, and lesser lights, as well as the
colonial amateur anthropolgists, Elliot, Crooke, and Ibbet-
son. Yet, strangely, in all the varied literature on the history, martial traditions, distribution, and customs of the
several Jat, Rajput, Bhuinhar, and Ahir "clans" spread
throughout Punjab, Uttar Pradesh, and Bihar, no clear
definition of "clan" appears, either in native Indian terms
or in anthropological terminology. Instead, "tribe," "clan,"
"family," and "lineage" are confusingly used by different
authors to refer to the same thing. Unfortunately, this
vagueness continues in recent research. Cohn limits his discussion to agnatic lineages which form talukas; yet agnatic
kinship ties were traced beyond the taluka boundary, and
the kin bodies usually termed "clans" in the earlier literature were clearly more complex institutions. K. N. Singh,
following Baden-Powell,[7] speaks of clans at the pargana

5. K. N. Singh, "The Territorial Basis of Medieval Town and
Village in Eastern Uttar Pradesh, India," *Annals of the Association
of American Geographers,* LVIII (1968), 208.

6. M. C. Pradhan, *The Political System of the Jats of Northern
India,* pp. 57ff.

7. Baden-Powell's discussion of the local organization of the clan
is adequate. At higher levels of kin organization, however, it
falters badly both conceptually and terminologically. See B. H.
Baden-Powell, *The Indian Village Community,* pp. 237–238.

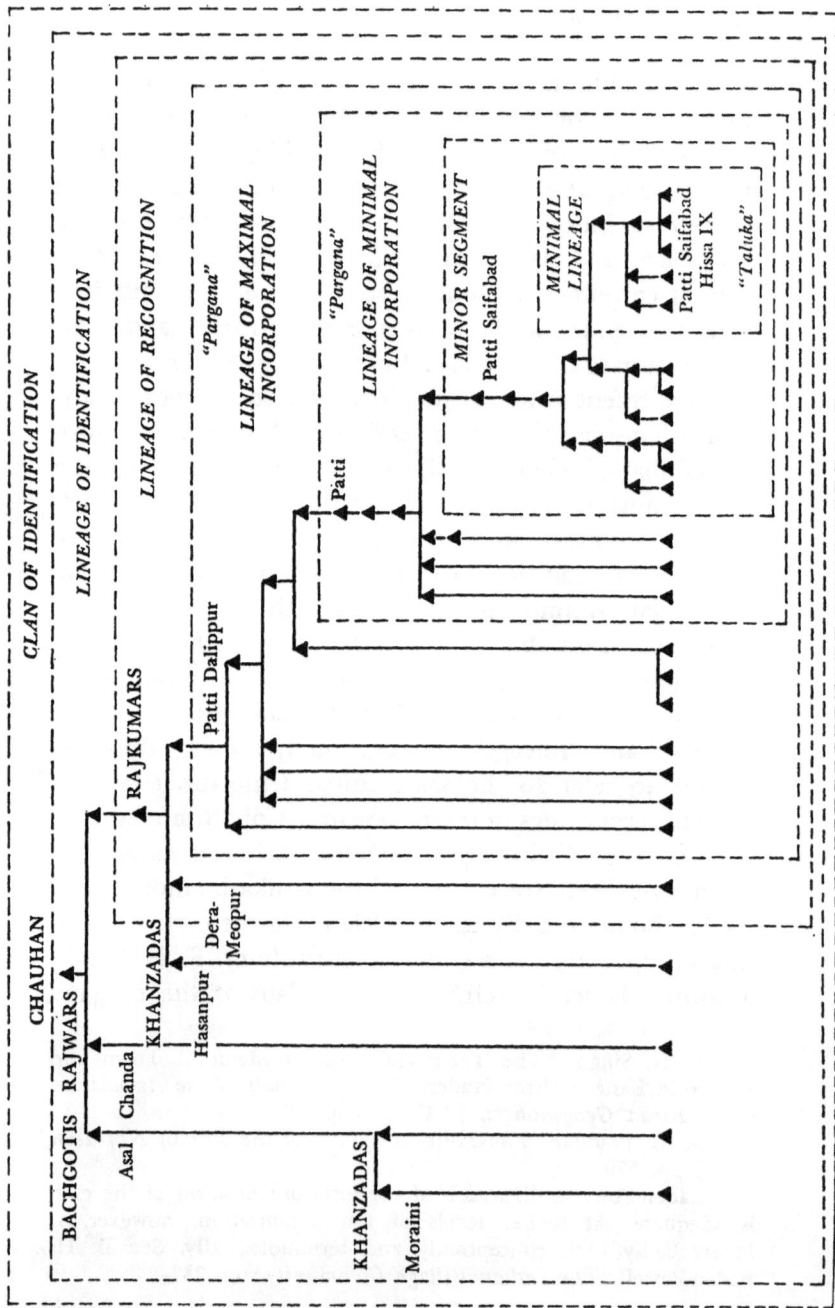

CHART 1: THE BACHGOTIS

level, "minor" clans, subclans or wider kindreds at the
tappa level, and close kindreds within the gaon. He also
speaks of "dominant Rajput lineages" which seem to be
kin bodies genealogically above and territorially beyond
the pargana clans, although exactly what they were Singh
does not specify.[8] Pradhan presents the most rigorous
classifications by dividing the Jats of a specific clan (clan
"Baliyan") into maximal lineages (thok), major segments
(sub-thok), and minimal lineages (khandan). The khandan,
sub-thok, and thok correspond to the lineage organization
within a single village, whereas the clan is dispersed over a
wide, although compact territory. Pradhan also applies the
term clan to a kinship grouping greater than the Baliyan
clan. This category, with which the Baliyans have unspe-
cified agnatic ties, is called the Kasshyap clan (got) and is
composed of several other clans similar to the Baliyan. The
Kasshyap clan is more dispersed territorially and seems
politically and behaviorally less significant than the "lesser"
clan.[9] Pradhan does not explain his terminological merger
of these seemingly distinctive levels of Jat kinship organization.

The confusing or contradictory terminology applied to
these "clans" is not wholly a matter of ethnographic naïvete.
Rather, the lack of precise definition mirrors the complex
social situation in which the kin groups were embedded,
a complexity born not of kinship structure but of the political and economic roles they performed in the state.

The cited authors all agree that kinship groups are significant political institutions in northern India. It remains,
however, to define precisely what these kin bodies are, and
at what territorial and genealogical level they are fitted
into the political apparatus of the preindustrial state.

The terminology applied to kinship groups in prein-

8. Singh, *op. cit.*, p. 208.
9. Pradhan, *op. cit.*, p. 59.

dustrial agrarian societies cannot simply be taken from anthropological analyses of primitive cultures. Morton H. Fried has shown how clan organization in preindustrial Chinese civilization was modified from that found in primitive societies to fit the exigencies of a complex (in Fried's terms, "stratified" state) society.[10] Also in India, membership in a lineage identified as Rajput was not necessarily a statement of historical genesis and genealogy. Rather, it was a claim to political status or a rationalization of political alliance. Because their internal cohesion and external recognition often hinged on political and economic roles in state administrative machinery, such kin bodies depended as much on political incorporation as genealogical continuity for their existence. What is true of the kin body also applies to the so-called caste. Presumed caste or varna [11] names such as Rajput, or Bhuinhar, or the more general Kshatriya, really refer to groups claiming similar social standing, similar attributional qualities [12] (including ceremonies or costumes as life style markers and genealogy), and similar political status. When local political kin bodies

10. Morton H. Fried, "The Classification of Corporate Unilineal Descent Groups," *Journal of the Royal Anthropological Institute of Great Britain and Ireland,* LXXXVII (1957), 15–16, 24.

11. The traditional all-India varna scheme consisted of four categories of castes (which have sometimes been mistaken for castes in their own right): the Brahman or priest, the Kshatriya or warrior-king, the Vaishya or cultivator and merchant-artisan, and the Sudra or menial-serf.

12. The dichotomy used throughout this essay between "attributional" and "interactional" follows McKim Marriott, "Attributional and Interactional Theories of Caste Ranking," *Man in India,* XXXIX (1959), 106–121 *passim.* "Attributional" similarities between groups refers to their sharing of common ideological motifs, of a common conceptual model with which they interpret or place themselves in the social order. "Interactional" similarities refers to direct political, economic, or military contact between groups. Groups sharing common attributes may be dispersed and noncorporate, while those which share interaction are close by each other and are politically or economically incorporated, or in corporate opposition to each other.

called themselves Rajput, they projected the same status and political image in terms of a supra-local category (often erroneously referred to as a caste) as was organized around nonfictive genealogical groups at a lower organizational level.

I speak here of an ideological model of genealogical descent which subsumed both local corporate kin bodies and dispersed, tenuous status categories with little direct behavioral significance. Dumont has shown that certain principles which regulate social behavior between castes in southern India, such as hierarchy, are important regulating principles within the kin groups of a single caste.[13] My point is similar, although kinship is regarded as primary and some aspects of caste are derived from it. Kinship which defines local Rajput corporate groups is by extension also able to bind nonresidential, noncorporate social units into a common attributional status category. Dumont speaks of a continuity of organizing principles between kin and caste in southern India. I note the emulation and duplication of an ideology of genealogical descent between local lineage and dispersed caste. Therefore, to understand caste, the unilineal kin bodies of which it is composed and which determined it must first be understood.

The descriptive terms applied to such kinship groups should specify their political and economic incorporation into the North Indian state, as well as their genealogical constitution. Following Fried's usage, I shall refer to the so-called clans of Rajputs, Jats, Bhuinhars, and other locally dominant Kshatriyas in northern India as "stratified lineages." "Stratified" means that these kin bodies are economically and politically differentiated.[14] The internal

13. Louis Dumont, *Hierarchy and Marriage Alliance in South Indian Kinship*, p. 4.

14. Fried, *op. cit.*, p. 26. For a more complete definition of stratification, see Morton H. Fried, *The Evolution of Political Society*, p. 57.

division of these lineages reflects the stratification throughout preindustrial Indian society. They are called lineages
instead of clans because the genealogical relationship between brethren can be traced, and because an individual's
relative genealogical position often determined internal organization, power, and political activities within these
groups.

A typical Rajput stratified lineage consisted of a demarcated although dispersed patrilineage of at least 6–8 generations. Chart 1 portrays the structural complexity and
multiple genealogical levels of a category of Rajput called
the Bachgotis. This highly ramified patrilineal descent
group originated from an ancestor, Barriar Singh, who
through guile or military prowess established his fortunes
in eastern Oudh at the end of effective Mughal rule. By
the late nineteenth century, various Bachgoti lines were
widely spread over much of eastern Oudh and the Banaras
districts including Faizabad, Sultanpur, Pratabgarh, and
Jaunpur districts. All Bachgotis can trace the exact genealogical steps which link them. They all also claim membership in a subcategory of Rajput status called the Chauhan clan. However, neither the terms Rajput, Chauhan, or
Bachgoti refer to the stratified lineage. In chart 1, the
Rajkumars of Patti Dalippur in Pratabgarh district of eastern Uttar Pradesh represent such a stratified lineage.[15]
Other Rajkumars in chart 1 (those of Dera-Meopur) are
not part of the Patti Dalippur stratified lineage even though

15. Chart I and maps 4 and 6 are derived in part from the Sultanpur and Faizabad settlement reports, and in part from the
Sultanpur Gazetteer. See H. R. Neville, *Sultanpur: A Gazetteer*,
genealogical appendices; A. F. Millett, *Settlement of the Land
Revenue of the Sultanpur District*, end maps, and A. F. Millett,
*Report of the Settlement of the Land Revenue of Fyzabad Dis-
trict*. Maps 2, 3, and 5 are modified from Oldham, *op. cit.*, end
maps and from D. T. Roberts, *Report on the Revision of Records
of Part of Ballia District*.

they share a common ancestor. Similarly, separate stratified lineages of Khanzadas, Rajwars, and Bachgotis (the
latter two internally divided into several stratified lineages) existed. All were included within the common category, Bachgotis, along with the Rajkumars. All shared a
common genealogy and exogamic rules. They did not,
however, form a single corporate kin unit. Their segmentation existed because the genealogical and territorial boundaries of the stratified lineage were determined as much by
their state political functions as by mere kin reckoning.

An alternative term for stratified lineage which would
define these state political functions is "lineage of maximal
political incorporation." The stratified lineage was the
widest kin body recognized within the administrative and
revenue organization of preindustrial North India. Such
political recognition by central authority was primarily
concerned with the collection of government land revenue
through the chiefs of the stratified lineage. Political recognition buttressed the self-definition, cohesion, and corporate activities of such lineages, and tended to make them
behaviorally, economically, and politically important to
their kin membership. This importance explains why genealogical connection may be recognized far beyond the
boundaries of corporate economic and political behavior
between kinsmen: the mandate of government is also
the mandate of kin allegiance. For this reason political
offices of hereditary kin leadership did not extend beyond
the stratified lineage even though genealogical connection
was so traced: the state-delegated powers of revenue collection and political action subsidize a local kin ruler and
elite. As Oldham notes:

The Mahomedan Government . . . often made the Rajah
or chief responsible for the land revenue of the whole tract
in the occupation of his clan; and thus by the recognition of

a supremacy already existing, helped to enforce and perpetuate it.[16]

Many of the early British revenue authorities understood this correlation between what they termed clan territories and low-level administrative or revenue localities such as the pargana, tappa, and taluka.[17] An example is the Bachgotis: originally the Rajkumars of Patti Dalippur (in chart 1) belonged to a single administrative unit whose boundaries were conterminous with those of the stratified lineage. This administrative division formed the pargana of Jelalpur Bilkhar in the Pratabgarh district, which existed until 1774. In that year, the Rajkumar estate and the administrative territory was partitioned between two sons into the separate parganas of Patti and Dalippur. In the revised revenue settlement of 1863, the British rejoined the two halves into the single pargana of Patti Dalippur, although their motive was administrative convenience rather than genealogical recognition.[18] K. N. Singh reports the existence of compact lineage teritories for the Rajputs of the Basti district in eastern Uttar Pradesh.[19] In the Ballia and Ghazipur districts of the Banaras region, the administrative division of the tappa (rather than the pargana) gen-

16. Wilton Oldham, *Historical and Statistical Memoir of the Ghazeepoor District*, part II, p. 43.

17. Cf. A. F. Millett, *Report of the Settlement of the Land Revenue of Fyzabad District*, para. 186; W. C. Benett, *Report of the Final Settlement of the Gonda District*, para. 68. Millett indicates that the boundaries of small Hindu states formed the basis of Muslim revenue division such as the pargana. See also Charles Alfred Elliott, *Chronicles of Oonao*, p. 149.

18. W. E. Forbes, *Report on the Revenue Settlement of the Partabgarh District*, p. 88.

19. Singh, *op. cit.*, p. 209; also see R. L. Singh and K. N. Singh, "Evolution of the Medieval Towns in the Saryu-par Plain of the Middle Ganga Valley: A Case Study," *The National Geographical Journal of India*, IX (1963), 2–6.

erally corresponded to the boundaries of a stratified lineage.[20]

Whether the boundaries of stratified lineages were conterminous with pargana or with tappa administrative divisions is unimportant. These administrative titles were applied to a local area by state design. A lineage dispersed
over a wide tract might merit incorporation as an independent pargana. A more compact lineage might be desig-
nated a tappa and be incorporated with other kin-defined
tappas into a pargana. The continuity between governmental boundary and kin territory is more important than
the administrative term applied. When the state is weak
and its administrative apparatus deficient, the bureaucratic
boundary coincides with the kin body. When the state is
strong, however, this coincidence is modified. Throughout
strong British rule in India, for example, administrative
divisions bore less and less relationship to Rajput kin divisions.

The relationship between pargana or tappa boundaries
and those of the stratified lineage is complex. Just as the
pargana originally may have been based on the distribution of a lineage, in later times, the lineage was defined by
the pargana. Even if, as often happened, the stratified lineage grew to exceed the boundaries of the pargana, it
would divide, so that the kin body of corporate behavior
still remained more or less within the boundaries of the
pargana or other administrative division. Map 3 indicates
the distribution of related stratified lineages over separate
tappas in the Ballia district. The distribution of the multiple stratified lineages contained within the Bachgoti category (see map 4) over several districts and many parganas
in Oudh and the Banaras region is another example.

Whether in any given instance it was the state which

20. See K. N. Singh's discussion of tappa and its relationship
to the pargana, *op. cit.*, p. 208.

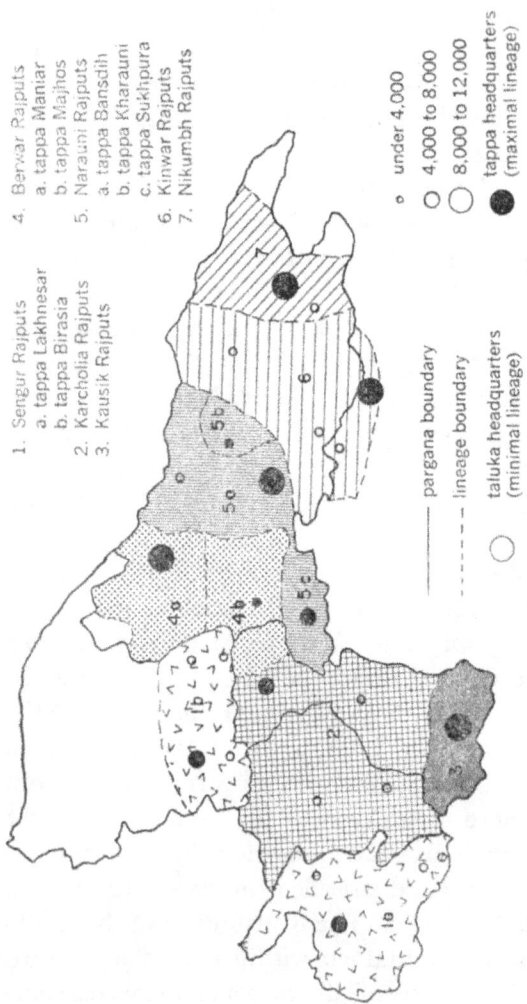

1. Sengur Rajputs
   a. tappa Lakhnesar
   b. tappa Birasia
2. Karcholia Rajputs
3. Kausik Rajputs

4. Berwar Rajputs
   a. tappa Maniar
   b. tappa Majhos
5. Narauni Rajputs
   a. tappa Bansdih
   b. tappa Kharauni
   c. tappa Sukhpura
6. Kinwar Rajputs
7. Nikumbh Rajputs

○ under 4,000
◯ 4,000 to 8,000
◯ 8,000 to 12,000
● tappa headquarters
  (maximal lineage)

——— pargana boundary
– – – lineage boundary
◯ taluka headquarters
  (minimal lineage)

MAP 3. **Related Stratified Lineage Distribution in Five Paraganas of Ballia District.** Different tappas within a single named kin group represent separate stratified lineages which retain recognition of common kinship. Tappa headquarters represent the residences of the stratified lineage elite. Taluka headquarters refer to residences of the leadership of lineages of minimal recognition. Compare the distribution of stratified lineages in Ballia with the undifferentiated distribution of Ballia lineages as portrayed in map 2.

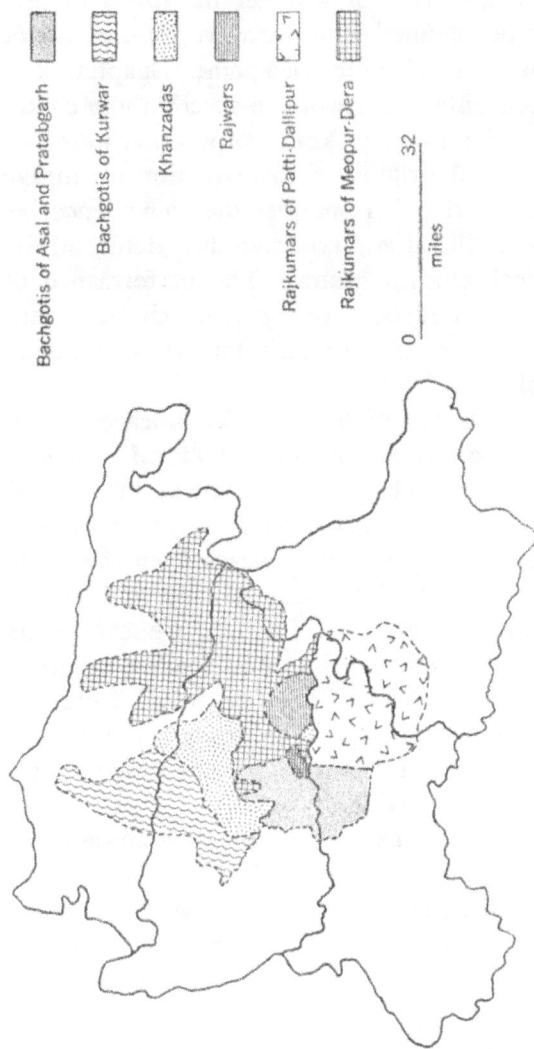

MAP 4. Distribution of the Bachgoti Category over Four Districts of Uttar Pradesh. The districts represented are Faizabad, Sultanpur, and the Pratabgarh districts in Oudh and the Jaunpur district in the Banaras region. (For the location of these districts, see map 1.) The distribution of the six major named categories comprising the Bachgotis is represented. Several of these categories were further internally divided into separate stratified lineages.

Legend:
- Bachgotis of Asal and Pratabgarh
- Bachgotis of Kurwar
- Khanzadas
- Rajwars
- Rajkumars of Patti-Dallipur
- Rajkumars of Meopur-Dera

0 _____ 32
miles

defined the kinship grouping as conterminous with pargana or tappa boundaries, or whether the limits of preexistent kin bodies defined administrative borders is not
significant from a synchronic viewpoint. Chapter four
adopts a developmental framework to specify those conditions where state definition or kin incorporation were primary. Whatever their origins, in this equation of lineage
with administrative division one sees the coincidence between state-level political and economic functions and the
structure of local kinship groups. The performance of
these functions and the local sovereignty which they entail
necessitates the preservation of such kin bodies and the
strengthening of their elites.

Exact genealogical age of the stratified lineage cannot
be specified because of the primacy of political events or
decisions at the state level rather than any solely internal
kinship process. Thus, the Khanzadas of Hasanpur in chart
1 broke off as a separate stratified lineage from the Bachgotis when their ancestor, Tatar Khan, a converted Hindu,
was shown favor by the court of Oudh. Genealogically
the Khanzadas of Moraini are the most shallow stratified
lineage within the Bachgotis. They separated from the
other groups to follow the path of political glory laid down
by the Khanzadas of Hasanpur, with whom, however, they
had little historical connection.

Great differences also existed in the geographical distribution and population of these lineages. Their geographical spread partly reflected the genealogical age of the
group, but it also mirrored success in military expansion
or grants of territory and preferment from the royal court.
(Compare the territorial extent of the different Bachgoti
stratified lineages in map 4 and those of Ballia district in
map 3.)

These patrilineages were internally stratified into socio-
economic classes which were usually consonant with the

genealogical rank of the individual. The closer in direct
line of patrilineal descent a person stood to the lineage
ancestor, the greater were his rank and political and economic powers. However, lineage stratification varied greatly
depending on the genealogical age, military success, size,
and relationship with the state of the kin group. These
variations are explained in terms of a developmental cycle
in the next chapter. In some areas a raja existed for the
entire stratified lineage whose status depended on primogenitural succession and impartible inheritance of the
family estate. Elsewhere rajas were absent, but chaudharis
or other such functionaries represented the stratified lineage in a more republican fashion. The office and role of
the stratified lineage leaders are discussed in the succeeding section of this chapter.

Each stratified lineage was divided into several sublin-
eages which also often performed significant political functions in the state. These "lineages of minimal political incorporation" tended to be the smallest corporate kinship
units recognized in the administrative structure of the
state. They corresponded to the administrative division of
the talukas (for example, note the stratified lineages inhabiting the several tappas of the Ballia district, each of
which is further divided into talukas. See map 3).

An example of the lineage of minimal incorporation is
the Rajkumars of Patti (in chart 1) during the period
when Jelalpur Bilkhar (Patti Dalippur) was the pargana
limit of the 'stratified lineage. However, when Patti and
Dalippur became separate parganas in 1774, the Patti
Saifabad "taluka" became the lineage of minimal political
incorporation within the pargana of Patti.[21] Toward the
close of the nineteenth century a further proprietary par-

21. Chart 1 attempts to show the developmental process by
indicating that both Patti and Patti Dalippur constituted the limits
of a pargana at different times.

tition in this estate took place when Patti Saifabad was divided into two new talukas. By this time, the British had revamped much of the former political and revenue system so that this change in proprietary arrangements at the local level was not precipitated by administrative changes at the pargana level. Throughout the British period the former concord between kin and administrative boundary increasingly tended to disappear, because of the proprietary upheavals which the British introduced, and because of the necessity for greater administrative efficiency. This disentanglement of kin and governmental bodies was not a unique occurrence or an aspect of the Westernization of India, but occurred whenever a strong central authority existed.

The corporate recognition by the state of the lineage of minimal incorporation was the result of land revenue engagement. Often the taluka as a unit was taxed, and the state took a lineage leader from this level as collection agent. The state had recourse to this alternative when it was strong enough to suppress the lineage raja and to attempt fragmentation of the stratified lineage. With success, this policy established the taluka as the level of the stratified lineage, and created a genealogically shallow and less populous kin body, more amenable to state control. This state strategy was strengthened when internal dissensions existed within the lineage, and when cadets of the main agnatic line threatened or attempted partition of the common patrimony. The lineage of minimal incorporation therefore often had hereditary rulers or representatives of genealogical status subordinate to the leaders of the whole stratified lineage, but nevertheless influential within their own kin jurisdictions.

Besides performing economic and political functions qualitatively similar to the functions of the entire stratified lineage, the lineage of minimal incorporation often became the seed for the formation of new stratified lineages. The founders of lineages of minimal incorporation were usually cadet lines descended from early generations of the main line of the stratified lineage. Such cadet lines were either assigned or managed to establish their own residential foothold and that of their followers in a number of villages. In the initial period of settlement, the lineage of minimal incorporation maintained its kinship and political ties with the stratified lineage leaders. In time, however, if events were favorable, the lineage of minimal incorporation established its own headquarters and threatened to become independent. This evolution eventually led to the fissioning of the lesser lineage. This happened to the Bachgotis several times in their history, and gave rise to the situation (portrayed in chart 1) of several independent stratified lineages, each with a history of common patrilineal descent, and each being able to define its exact genealogical relationship to any other.

Below the lineage of minimal incorporation came the minor lineage segment. Several minor lineages resided in a single village and were usually equivalent to the revenue divisions called *pattis*. Unless they could claim descent from a lineage leader in a recent generation, their internal divisions were not important outside the village except when land revenue settlements were made with a *mukaddam* (headman) or village leader representing the local minor lineage. Several such representatives often lived in a single village. Mukaddams were charged with revenue collection when the state attempted to bypass the stratified lineage raja and elite. Rather than being the lowest level of lineage incorporation, the minor lineage as revenue payer represents the successful abrogation by central authority of stratified lineage preeminence and political power.

The lowest-level of lineage segmentation was the minimal

lineage of three to six generations. This kin level was also the most important because in each stratified lineage one minimal lineage provided the raja, chaudhari, or other elite membership of the kin body. Where this delegation did not exist, the stratified lineage had reached a stage in its development when political control had passed out of its hands and an egalitarianism of mediocrity occurred.

I pass now to a consideration of genealogical groupings geographically and structurally more widespread than the stratified lineage. From this discussion it will become clear how localized, corporate kin groups give way to increasingly tenuous social categories until the social institutions commonly identified as caste and varna appear.

When fission occurred in a stratified lineage, the ties of patrilineal kinship which once bound the separate groups were remembered. Often, such fission led to hostility between the previously unified segments. At other times, the segments would form into mutually opposed factions. A third possibility was the maintenance of military and political cooperation. The Bachgotis with their several internal divisions, and the multi-tappa organization of the Sengur, Berwar, and Narauni Rajputs of Ballia (see maps 3 and 4), are such suprastratified lineage groupings. These larger categories of lineage identity have often been mistaken as the important limits of corporate kin and political behavior and thus been confused with the stratified lineage level.

Characteristic of these more inclusive levels of kin organization was their greater immunity from the fissioning process which conditioned the continuous formation of new kin groups at the stratified lineage level and below. When the Rajkumar pargana of Jelalpur Bilkhar splits into Patti and Dalippur, two separate kin bodies appear. However, they remain Rajkumars. No matter how many separate stratified lineages evolve, they will probably retain with great tenacity their identification as Rajkumars. This greater stability with respect to the formal identity of higher-order kin categories increases in scale from local to highly dispersed kin groupings, that is, in the passage from corporate group up to attributional category. Genealogical points or levels, therefore, exist where the kin segmentation process ends, where the purely interactional aspect of kin relations and its dynamism based on fission stops, and is replaced by a stereotyped genealogical referent or identity.

Independent stratified lineages which retained memory of their former genealogical connection and which interacted, I have termed a "lineage of (maximal) recognition." These lineages shared two common qualities: they usually recognized a common name, and they normally did not permit intermarriage within their component groups. For example, in chart 1 the Rajkumars of Patti Dalippur and the Rajkumars of Meopur and Dera are separate stratified lineages which, however, trace their descent back to a common ancestor, have a common name (Rajkumar) and proscribe the intermarriage of their members. Other lineages of maximal recognition shown in chart 1 are the Rajwars and Bachgotis (the latter retaining the original name of the entire kin line). The lineage of maximal recognition is sometimes referred to in the literature as the "major clan" or "tribe." However, it was not politically and economically defined by revenue collection for the state as was the stratified lineage or the lineage of minimal incorporation. Therefore, the extent of political cooperation, the nature of status prerogatives, and the leadership within the lineage of recognition were at a reduced level.

The extant literature is not enlightening regarding the social functions of this level of genealogical reckoning. Determining what specific lineage grouping the British commentators were referring to in their ill-defined terminology of "clans," "tribes," and "races" is an additional difficulty. The data available almost invariably portray the relationship between the stratified lineages composing a lineage of recognition as hostile. Their conflicts generally concerned division of and control over once joint patrimonial territory. In a sense, such competition between closely related stratified lineages is the counterpart of the conflict between senior elite and cadet lines within a single stratified lineage. Political cooperation or meaningful offices of leadership at this level of Rajput kin reckoning were rare.

For example, Oldham reports a long-standing conflict between the several actual or would-be tappas of the Narauni Rajputs in the Ballia district.[22] Within the Bachgoti category of Rajkumars, the houses of Dera and Meopur were constantly at odds. These two talukas formed independent stratified lineages, and joined the Rajkumars of Patti Dalippur to form a common lineage of recognition. In their dispute, the houses of Dera and Meopur were joined by their close agnates, representing cadet branches which had received small shares of the original patrimony. Most of the disputes concerned proprietary rights over villages which had once been jointly controlled.[23]

Other evidence suggests a somewhat less antagonistic relationship within a lineage of recognition. Sleeman reports that the Raja of Tulsipur was offered aid in a political contest by neighboring rajas and others of high status who were his distant kinsmen. The same author notes that although Rajputs might be in grave conflict among themselves, they would invariably join together to meet an external threat.[24] More important, however, the greatest and most frequent threats to a stratified lineage came from its

22. Oldham, *op. cit.*, part I, p. 94.
23. H. R. Neville, *Sultanpur: A Gazetteer,* p. 84.
24. W. H. Sleeman, *A Journey Through the Kingdom of Oude in 1849–50,* I, 37.

close agnates composing a common lineage of recognition.

In some of the largest kin groups, another lineage level, above the lineage of recognition, became established. This "lineage of identification" also shared the common name, although its constituent units may have intermarried freely, sometimes in hypergamous fashion. The Bachgotis of chart 1 are a lineage of identification divided into Rajwar, Rajkumar, and Bachgoti lineages of maximal recognition. The maintenance (or creation) of this lineage tie seems in large measure dictated by status considerations and demands. Fictive kin ties are found throughout the kin bodies of Uttar Pradesh. Because the ties binding the lineage of identification were those of status (or status claims) and not solely kinship or geographical proximity, such ties could be denied.

In the last avowedly genealogical cateogry, the "clan of identification," kinship and genealogical connection are reduced to unimportance in relation to what is clearly a unit of status and prestige. Because their genealogies were vaguely specified and because kinship merely rationalized the connection of such categories rather than creating them, I call this level a "clan." An example is the "Chauhan" Rajput, a category to which all the Bachgotis diagramed in chart 1 claimed to belong. This Chauhan allegiance merged them with other kin bodies distributed through Uttar Pradesh and other states. In 1901 the Chauhan population was 461,706 and the Bachgoti (of all types) 35,992.[25] "Chauhan," then, is a category aligning many disparate Rajput groupings, each of which claims similar historical origins and a similar regional prestige rating. The term "Bais" appears to be another example of a Rajput clan of identification. H. M. Elliot lists the Bais as "one of 36 royal races of Rajputs," and locates them in

25. W. Crooke, *Tribes and Castes of the Northwestern Provinces,* IV, 216.

such distant districts as Budaon, Mainpuri, Aligarh, Eta-
wah, and Kanpur in western Uttar Pradesh and Allahabad,
Azamgarh, Gorakhpur, Ghazipur, and Jaunpur of eastern
Uttar Pradesh.[26]

A few dozen such clans of identification comprised the
entire population of Rajputs in northern India. They were
arranged in a linear rank order which often served as the
justification for the hypergamy practiced by local kin
groups. A lineage of interaction claiming Chauhan status
might only send their women in marriage to nearby kin
bodies claiming a higher clan identification. Clan status,
like the hypergamous marriage rules, was in genealogical
terms a claim to common status and thus an aspect of political alliance. This political process and status usually applied only in a very local territory. The hypergamous system did not necessarily operate regionally. Bais Rajputs
who hypergamously married with Chauhans in one locale
might not intermarry with Chauhans from another. Indeed, the status of all Rajputs declined as one moved from
west to east.

The Rajput clan of identification is the most dispersed
and least interacting of all kin bodies so far described. It is
therefore most dependent on shared status (or claims to
shared status) and emulation of various Chauhan or Bais
insignia, including a fictive genealogy. The Rajput clan
of identification is also the kin tie most easily denied and
most difficult to substantiate except in terms of local prestige and status. Elliott reports that the Raikwars of Oonao
claimed kinship with the famous Raikwar Rajas of Bah-
raich, but their claim was not accepted until they began
to rise in local political status.[27] Benett reports that among

26. H. M. Elliot, *Memoirs on the History, Folklore, and Distribution of the Races of the North-Western Provinces of India,*
I, 8.

27. Elliott, *op. cit.,* p. 44.

the Bisen Rajputs, the ties of clanship were weak because the Bisen chief of Majhauli (Gorukhpur) would not eat with the chiefs of Gonda or Pratabgarh.[28] Claims to clan membership might be buttressed by behavior rather than merely ideological avowal. The Neikumbh Rajputs of Kharid pargana of the Ballia district claim descent from Raja Akhraj Deo of Oonwal in Gorukhpur district. Oldham notes that they were anxious to maintain their kin ties, and had sent their headman to plant trees and dig wells in Gorukhpur at the end of the eighteenth century.[29] Avowals of clan membership might be used to alter the hypergamous marriage circle of a Rajput lineage of recognition. In such instances, the local grouping consciously pursued the designation, status, and renown of a supralocal category through claims of common descent. The clan of identification thus stood at the very limit of genealogical attribution in the formation of political or status categories. The clan of identification completes the passage upward from the local, corporate stratified lineage and its even more local components to the diffuse, attributional, quasi-genealogical categories of Rajput lineality. Caste and varna emerge as elements of this lineage scheme.

The organization of castes depended on the level of the lineage of recognition. Several lineages of recognition hypergamously intermarried within a geographical region defined by availability of transportation and communication as well as formal rules of village exogamy and prescription of marital direction. This zone of intermarriage thus formed an endogamous, commensally equivalent, and mutually ranked social group. These qualities also define a caste. The Rajkumars of Meopur-Dera and Patti Dalippur coupled with all the nearby lineages of recognition

28. W. C. Benett, *Report of the Final Settlement of the Gonda District,* para. 33.
29. Oldham, *op. cit.,* part I, p. 60.

CHART 2: THE RAJPUT LINEAGE HIERARCHY

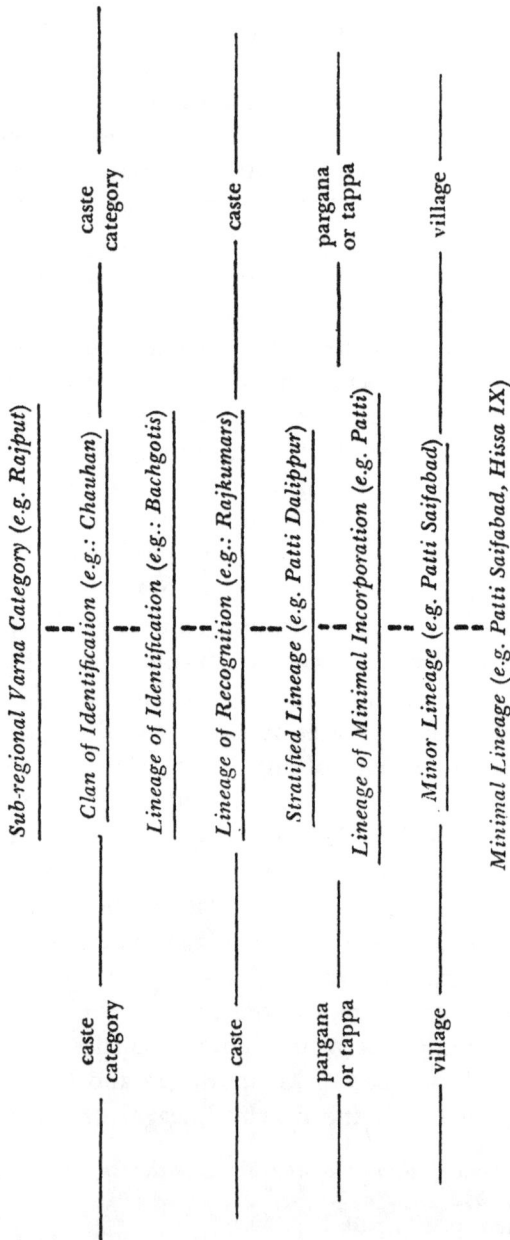

Sub-regional Varna Category (e.g. Rajput)		
————— caste category		
	Clan of Identification (e.g.: Chauhan)	————— caste category
	Lineage of Identification (e.g.: Bachgotis)	
————— caste	*Lineage of Recognition (e.g.: Rajkumars)*	————— caste
	Stratified Lineage (e.g. Patti Dalippur)	
————— pargana or tappa	*Lineage of Minimal Incorporation (e.g. Patti)*	————— pargana or tappa
	Minor Lineage (e.g. Patti Saifabad)	
————— village	*Minimal Lineage (e.g. Patti Saifabad, Hissa IX)*	————— village

A caste category includes a single dispersed clan of identification. A caste includes several dispersed lineages of recognition which form an endogamous region. A pargana or tappa includes a single stratified lineage or lineage of minimal incorporation. A village consists of several co-resident minor lineages.

with which they married thus formed a local endogamous caste (see charts 1 and 2).

The literature is unclear on how two lineages of recognition claiming a common clan of identification regulated marriage. Did some Chauhans marry other Chauhans? Did the "Bais" of one region intermarry wtih their clan fellows elsewhere? Elliot reports that the Bhadauriyas, a former branch of the Chauhan Rajputs, denied this genealogy after intermarrying with Chauhans.[30] But Elliot does not state who or where these Chauhans were with whom the Bhadauriya Rajputs intermarried. Perhaps the clan of identification might best be conceptualized as a caste category or caste cluster whose component groups were not endogamous. Bailey defines a caste category as an aggregate

of persons, usually in the same linguistic region, usually with the same traditional occupation and sometimes with the same caste name. These are not social strata since, while they are exhaustive . . . and exclusive . . . they are not unambiguously groups. They are categories made up of groups with similar attributes.[31]

Rajput organization differs in that categories such as Chauhan were not composed of endogamous local castes, but rather comprised lineages of recognition hypergamously linked with other local, non-Chauhan groups. Just as endogamy is a guarantor of caste purity and a buttress to caste self-definition, hypergamy is a way of spreading political alliances over regions and of organizing disparate groups around a common status system. Orenstein notes the weakness of caste organization among the Mahrattas, a locally dominant population similar to the Rajputs.[32]

30. Elliot, *op. cit.*, p. 25.

31. Bailey, *op. cit.*, p. 107. For the similar concept of a "caste cluster," see Iravati Karve, *Hindu Society: An Interpretation*, p. 10.

32. Henry Orenstein, "Caste and the Concept, 'Mahratta,' in Maharasthra," *Eastern Anthropologist*, XVI (1963), 1–9.

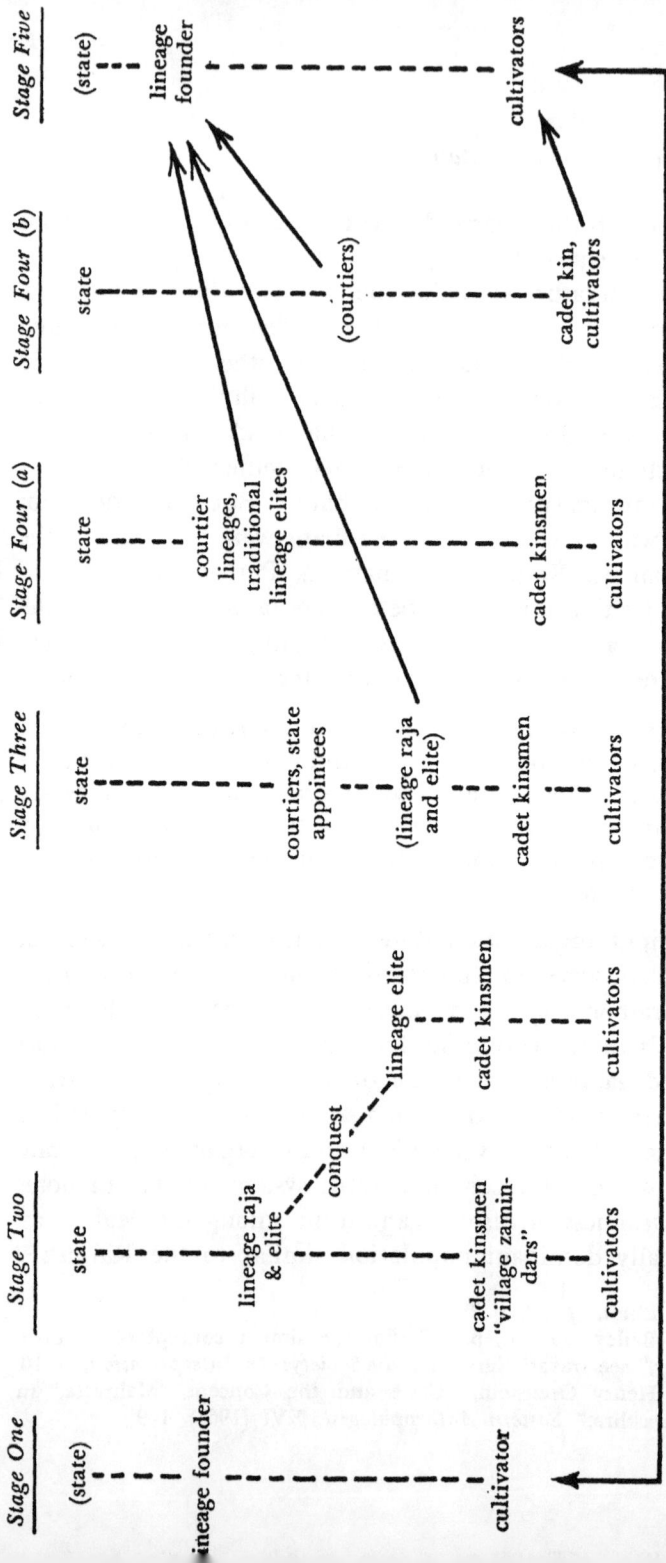

CHART 3: DEVELOPMENT CYCLE OF THE RAJPUT LINEAGE

Relative strength of the various segments of the political order within each stage is indicated by variable lengths of the dotted lines. A parenthesis indicates that this group was either weak or nonexistent during this period. Solid lines indicate the origin of one group from another in the succession of developmental stages. Stage five represents the regeneration of the cycle and the early phases of stage one.

The clan of identification is not so clearly demarcated in structure as the equivalent caste category found in non-dominant categories. This looseness may be an index of the political alliance and attributional emulation of status created over regions by the *de jure* hypergamy of categories such as Chauhan or Bais. Chart 3 attempts to portray the organization of the local caste and caste category in terms of the genealogical structure of the Rajput kin body.

Caste as defined by the lineage of recognition is a further extension of the unilineal kin pattern with the addition of affinity (prohibitions or prescriptions concerning marriage). Caste has usually not been seen as depending on this level of social structure. Rather, categories such as Rajput, Jat, Bhuinhar, have been treated as castes. Undoubtedly, within a single village community, all people calling themselves Jat or Rajput belonged to the same locally endogamous caste group. To take such names as indicative of a single regional caste would miss, however, important aspects of Indian social structure.

I argued elsewhere that Rajput and similar locally dominant groupings were categories composed of many disparate and dispersed local castes and caste categories.[33] Such castes and caste categories were united only in their claim to a common attributional status, rank, and perhaps traditional occupation, and they all generally followed a common attributional life style defined as Rajput (or other locally recognized status term such as Mahratta or Jat). I referred to such categories as "subregional varna categories." The latter are one organizational step beyond the caste and caste category. Unlike the caste, subregional varna categories are geographically dispersed and have few or no corporate activities. Unlike the caste category, they

33. See Richard G. Fox, "Varna Schemes and Ideological Integration in Indian Society," *Comparative Studies in Society and History*, XI (1969), 27–45.

are composed of disparate groups with only the most tenuous claims to a common ancestry, status, and social behavior. The component units of the subregional varna category merely emulate the model of a Rajput, Jat, or Bhuinhar which they derive from real Rajputs, Jats, Bhuinhars in their local area. Clearly, the stated contention must be further researched. However, even today in village India, many unrelated castes claim the name of a locally dominant caste or caste category.[34] It would seem that such claims would have been a vehicle of social mobility of more direct behavioral consequence in rural life than claims to higher standing in the all-India varna scheme. Admission to Kshatriya varna standing in a local area said less interactionally for a mobile caste than admission to the status of Rajputs in a region controlled by Rajputs, or Jats, in a region where Jats were dominant.

Other scattered evidence suggests this hypothesis. In some parts of Uttar Pradesh, several neighboring lineages of recognition exist in which one group claims to be Rajput and the other Bhuinhar. For example, the Sukurwars found mainly in Zamaneah pargana of the Ghazipur district trace their descent back to a mythical Godh Raja. This raja is said to have had four sons, from which all present Sukurwar lines descended. The descendants of three of the sons are still known as Bhuinhars, the designation of Godh Raja. The descendants of the fourth son are known either as Rajputs, Bhuinhars, or Muslims depending on their particular lineage.[35] Similarly, the Kinwars of Mahomedabad and Dehma parganas in Ghazipur are known as Bhuinhars, while those of nearby Kharid pargana in Ballia are considered Rajputs (see map 5).[36] Further, indigenous groups which called themselves "Bhumia

34. *Ibid.*, p. 33.
35. Oldham, *op. cit.*, part I, pp. 61–64.
36. *Ibid.*, p. 60.

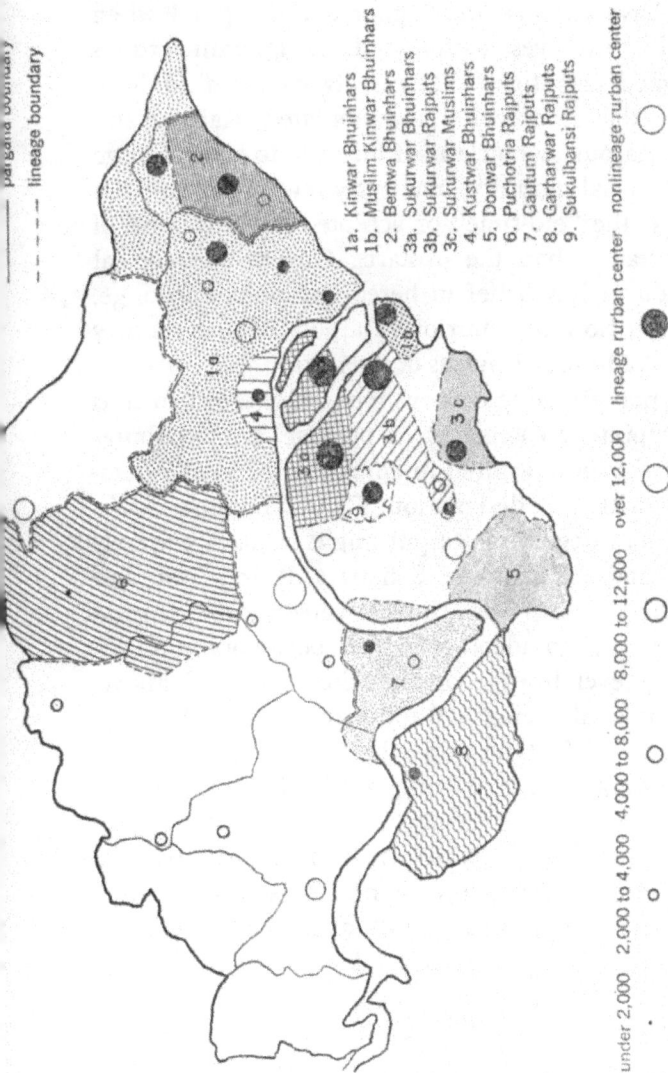

--- pargana boundary
---- lineage boundary

1a. Kinwar Bhuinhars
1b. Muslim Kinwar Bhuinhars
2. Bemwa Bhuinhars
3a. Sukurwar Bhuinhars
3b. Sukurwar Rajputs
3c. Sukurwar Muslims
4. Kustwar Bhuinhars
5. Donwar Bhuinhars
6. Puchotria Rajputs
7. Gautum Rajputs
8. Garharwar Rajputs
9. Sukulbansi Rajputs

under 2,000   2,000 to 4,000   4,000 to 8,000   8,000 to 12,000   over 12,000   lineage rurban center   nonlineage rurban center

MAP 5. Lineage Distribution and Rurban Centers in Ghazipur District. The contiguous distribution of kin categories which claim distinct subregional varna allegiances is shown for the Kinwars and the Sukurwars. Lineage rurban centers refer to the urban-like communities where the lineage elite resided. The distribution of such rurban centers reflects the location of lineages rather than a locational pattern based on random distribution of equidistant dispersion. Parganas without lineages have fewer and smaller rurban centers than those with lineages. Compare their distribution and size with map 2 of Ballia district. (For the location of Ghazipur district within Uttar Pradesh, see map 1.)

Rajputs" are mentioned in the old revenue literature. The latter may have adopted the cognomen, "Rajput," when they found themselves surrounded by migrant groups which claimed this title.[37] There always seem to have been "real" (that is, accepted and emulated) Rajputs and others, non-Rajputs, who claimed this title to gain prestige and perhaps social mobility. The early revenue authorities believed that the "old-time" or accepted Rajputs were of a different stamp than the upstarts. Greater sociological sophistication or less belief in hereditary noblesse oblige, might explain how the spurious Rajputs of one century became the "old-time" Rajputs of the next.

If this hypothesis should prove true, then terms such as "Rajput" represent categories of prestige and attributes to which local groups aspired in emulation of locally dominant castes with this designation. Castes claiming a subregional varna category of Rajput might in other contexts or at other times claim to be Kshatriya. Rajput, Jat, and Bhuinhar membership was a further categorical extension of the same kinship ideology which behaviorally incorporated local-level lineage organization described above. For the individual, being a Rajkumar of Patti Dalippur affected his daily life, land ownership, personal protection, and local prestige, whereas being a Chauhan Rajput impinged little on social existence. In this sense, the Rajkumar status is more behaviorally "real" than the Chauhan status. But direct social reality is not the sole issue. The patrilineal ideology of kin status which mandated the Rajkumars also defined the Chauhans. This chain of ideological emulation (centered on principles of descent) links locality and region as it links stratified lineage to clan of identification. The interaction between this ideology of kinship and the actual political organization of the North Indian state will become clear in chapter five.

37. Benett, *op. cit.,* para. 33.

This section has identified one of the linkages between local communities and the larger society. The genealogical forms which define the local stratified lineage also fashion the caste and subregional varna category. There is, however, another linkage. This linkage is not concerned with the sharing of attributes of structure or forms from local community to larger society; rather it concerns the direct interaction between central authority and the pivotal figure of the stratified lineage, the raja.

THE RAJA

The elite of a stratified lineage [38] were called rajas, chaudharis, talukdars or babus and usually inherited their prerogatives of power and influence, either as autocratic leaders or republican representatives of their kin groups. Often, genealogies were carefully maintained as proof of their right to office. They were, undoubtedly, just as carefully fabricated when changed political realities so demanded. The lineage leadership acted as a hinge linking the local stratified lineage with state authority. The state used them to collect the land revenue due in the lineage territory, a privilege which conferred upon the lineage elite great autonomy and local power. Their kin brethren viewed them as paramount in rank and wealth within the lineage and provided the substance of their military following. At times, both the kin body and the state attempted to circumvent the elite and replace them with a more direct channel between local community and state power. In turn, the lineage elite manipulated both their kin obligations and following as well as their state duties in order to cement their superiority over their kinsmen

38. From this point forward, when the term, "lineage," is employed without a modifier, the reference will always be to a "stratified lineage."

and to maintain local autonomy from the state. For example, when the raja in his role of revenue engager (or payer) was strong, he would commonly try to strip his lineage mates of their proprietary rights and reduce them to undertenants.

The lineage elite formed a minimal lineage 3–6 generations old. The size of this group varied directly with the power of the lineage head: when he was strong, he had many relatives; when he was weak, his close relatives partitioned their estates from his and became threats to his position. Only such minimal lineages which could trace their descent back directly to the lineage ancestor were economically or politically significant. Other, cadet lineages, were either quickly reduced to the level of the rest of the lineage brethren, or were successful in starting an independent stratified lineage of their own.

Sometimes the stratified lineage as a whole had to ratify the genealogical candidate for lineage raja. At other times, the assembled lineage directly elected a kin leader. Primogenitural succession to lineage leadership was a third possibility. I am not here interested in the mechanics of selection or the title given the lineage head, but rather in the powers and obligations of the lineage leader and his relation to his lineage mates. The following pages will therefore generally refer to a lineage elite, rather than a particular raja or chaudhari. This plural terminology is used because the minimal partrilineage of the kin leader normally resided with him in the lineage center or in close-by villages allowed them for their maintenance. This corporate kin group buttressed the status and power of the lineage head, provided his "court," took part in the management of the common property, and basked in his reflected glory.

The lineage elite did not own the land of their lineage, although they were often called upon by the state to pay the land revenue for the whole region, as well as revenue due from their actual holdings. Proprietary rights—or more correctly, managerial rights over land—were more fragmented than political and kinship alliances. But where managerial rights over land overlapped with the interests of the state—as in the collection of land revenue—the lineage elite had important executive powers. These powers emerged not from the kinship web of the lineage elite, but from the delegation of tax-collecting functions by the state. Therefore, when the state was strong, it attempted to set aside the lineage elite as revenue intermediaries and to deal directly with individual segments of the kin body (usually minor lineages of a village or village group.)

S. N. Hasan has referred to what I here call the lineage elite as "intermediary zamindars," and their kin following as "primary zamindars." [39] Similarly, P. C. Wheeler earlier talked of "goshwara" or pargana zamindars (as opposed to village zamindars) who collected land revenue for the entire pargana although they owned only small segments of it.[40] This revenue collection policy is important because it shows that at all levels lineage brethren and elite held superior proprietary rights over actual cultivators. Sometimes members of the kin body were also cultivators—particularly in highly ramified, land-poor stratified lineages—in which case, they usually held their lands at state revenue rates lower than cultivators not of the kin group.[41]

In a typical village of eastern Uttar Pradesh, four levels

39. S. Nurul Hasan, "The Position of the Zamindars in the Moghul Empire," *Indian Economic and Social History Review,* I (1964), 114. See also S. Nurul Hasan, "Zamindars Under The Mughals," *Land Control and Social Structure in Indian History,* pp. 19–29.

40. P. C. Wheeler, *Revision of Records and Settlement Operations in Jaunpur District,* para. 178.

41. Millett, *op. cit.* (1880), para. 219; see also John Thomason, *Report of the Collector of Azimgurh on the Settlement of the Ceded Portion of the District Commonly called Chuklah Azimgurh,* p. 14.

of traditional land holding or engagement in agricultural production could be distinguished. The highest ranking and wealthiest village segment consisted of the resident members of the Rajput stratified lineage. These are often referred to in British revenue literature as "village zamindars." A typical village did not contain representatives of the stratified lineage elite. These lived in the lineage urban center (see below). Ranking below the village zamindars in power and proprietary tenure came the resident occupancy tenants. The latter cultivated village lands not in direct use by the village zamindars. Resident tenants were often the remnants of former classes of village zamindars now depressed to the level of common cultivators and dispossessed of all proprietary or managerial discretion over the lands they worked. Below the resident cultivators stood the nonresident tenants who came from nearby villages to cultivate lands seasonally. At the very bottom stood the landless laborers of low caste who were employed as plowmen and field laborers on the directly cultivated fields (so-called "sir" lands as opposed to those given out to tenants) of the village zamindars.[42] The succeeding chapter will discuss how the variable fortunes of stratified lineages often reduced elites to the status of village zamindars, or in more depressed circumstances, lowered their lineage brethren from village zamindars to common resident cultivators. The several levels of power and land control were relatively static within an Indian village; what altered greatly over time were the specific occupants of each village rank.

The lineage elite was pivotal in organizing protection for their lineage mates, in constructing and maintaining various social amenities, and in subsidizing the ritual life of their kin following. The raja or chaudhari and his

42. Sulekh Chandra Gupta, *Agrarian Relations and Early British Rule in India*, pp. 38–39.

minimal lineage, retainers, and agricultural tenantry inhabited a mud fort which was the focus of the lineage. These centers often had "rurban," or urban-like, characteristics. Kinsmen retreated to this fort in times of attack or to escape the avaricious state revenue collector. Such fortifications often also protected the lineage elite from dissident cadet lines or kin brethren.[43] Cadet lines became residentially separate when no more room existed in the fort. The raja or chaudhari then settled a cadet line in other villages (usually nearby) so that they would pose no threat to his command. Rajput mud forts throughout Oudh formed the principal military opposition to British armies during the conclusion of the Mutiny of 1857.[44] Earlier these forts acted as formidable obstacles to the East India Company's attempted pacification of the Doab between 1805–1816.[45] The lineage fort of the raja was also sometimes the ritual center for the kin brotherhood. The size and territorial distribution of lineage rurban centers is indicated in map 2 of the Ballia District and map 5 of the Ghazipur district.

The lineage elite also built temples, ponds, and supervised the economic and agricultural development of their lineage territories. They subsidized markets in the rural

43. The analysis of the role of lineage elites in the formation of urban-like settlements is discussed in Richard G. Fox, "Rurban Centers and Rajput 'Clans' in Northern India," in R. G. Fox ed., *Urban India: Society, Space, and Image* (in press).

44. John William Kaye, *History of the Sepoy War of 1857–58*, III, 191, 195–196.

45. Thakur Dya Ram of Hattrass was a lineage head in the Aligarh district whom the British feared and placated in the early days of their occupation of the Doab. Finally in 1816 when the British became more confident, and when Dya Ram's political independence became increasingly noxious, the East India Company troops attacked and leveled the thakur's mud fort. See J. R. Hutchinson, *Allyghur Statistics, Being a Report on the General Administration of that District from A.D. 1803 to the Present Time*, pp. 17–18.

areas. Often the size of a market depended less on its com-
mercial functions than on the prestige of its lineage spon-
sor and his attempts to raise his prestige. The lineage elite
may also have played a role in determining caste rankings
within their kinship and political jurisdictions.

The military threat of a lineage elite depended on the
lower-ranking kinsmen who formed the majority of their
army. In the literature, a great deal of argument sur-
rounds the nature of military service by lineage members.
One group of scholars sees such military service as a matter of kin obligation. Benett writes of a lineage leader
gathering "the militia levies of his clansmen and their dependents for the prosecution of his private disputes or at
the summons of the chieftain of his tribe." [46] He further
notes that "when the raja went to war he was followed
by an enthusiastic army attached to himself and to each
other by the closest ties of common origin and common interests." [47] On the other hand, Millett believed that kinsmen did not owe military duties to the lineage head.
Therefore, when such services were rendered, they were
compensated with money. According to Millett, a lineage
head had to maintain soldiers, and by employing his kinsmen he fulfilled an obligation to support his lineage
brethren.[48] This argument might be resolved by recognizing that at different stages in a stratified lineage's development, military cooperation depended on kin obligation or
on internal economic stratification.

The distinction between the autocratic leadership of
highly stratified lineages and the republican representatives of a more egalitarian kin body is often made in the
literature. These two forms of the lineage are seen as ex-

46. W. C. Benett, *A Report on the Family History of the Chief
Clans of the Roy Bareilly District*, para. 74.

47. Benett, *op. cit.* (1870), para. 75.

48. A. F. Millett, *Settlement of the Land Revenue of the Sultanpur District*, para. 157.

clusive. In fact, they represent opposite poles on a continuum of rank, power, and state favor. Given certain
ecological conditions and state relations, lineages produced
powerful, almost despotic kin rulers. Under other political
and environmental circumstances, a smaller power gap existed between lineage elite and their kin brotherhood. In
some situations, lineages without rajas developed them;
more commonly, lineages with an hereditary elite were reduced to a socially undifferentiated and unstratified condition. To discover in depth what circumstances produced
each of these types is the concern of the succeeding chapter.
The lineage elite transmitted its values, decrees, military
call-ups, and political duties to a body of subordinate kinsmen. Sometimes the latter were inferior in real power,
sometimes inferior only in status, but always they were
bound to the elite by kinship obligation and kinship etiquette.

Similarly, the relationship of lineage elite and the state
was based on delegated power from above, the balance of
which at times lay with the state, at other times with the
lineage elite. This balance greatly influenced the nature of
the lineage elite and its relationship with the larger kin
group. However, whether state or lineage elite power was
stronger, each institution was forced to recognize the
other—if no more than in an attempt to rid itself of that
burden.

THE STATE

The following investigation of the central authority under
which kin and raja flourished is limited to its influence on
the local-level political organization and the institutions of
lineages and their elites.

R. E. Frykenberg has noted that the Western concept
of the state is not readily applicable to governmental forms

in traditional India.[49] The state in Western political theory enjoys a monopoly of coercive force in the society, and is the center of administrative decisions and judicial review. Frykenberg suggests that traditional polities in South Asia never controlled such centralized powers. Rather, administration, police, and civil activities often were dispersed, sometimes resting with the virtually autonomous or independent local overlords, and at other times with kin groups or civil servants.

Walter Neale has noted a similar situation in terms of the productive process in traditional northern India.[50] He shows that many levels of local, regional, and finally central power holders interceded between the cultivator and state authority. Neale indicates how each power stratum in the society had a share of the grainheap allocated to it, and how the power equilibrium of the polity was reflected in the distribution of the peasant's productivity. Bernard Cohn and A. M. Shah [51] have analyzed the levels of political organization during the eighteenth century in the Banaras region and Gujarat, respectively. Cohn speaks of four levels:

a) Imperial: The Mughal empire in the eighteenth century represented this level. Even rebellious local elements during this period of Mughal decline sought acceptance and accreditation by the imperial power to justify their power seizure.

b) Secondary: This realm exercised sovereignty over a major cultural and historical region (such as Oudh or Bengal).

49. Robert Eric Frykenberg, "Traditional Processes of Power in South India: An Historical Analysis of Local Influence," *Indian Economic and Social History Review*, I (1963), 136.

50. Walter C. Neale, *Economic Change in Rural India: Land Tenure and Reform in Uttar Pradesh, 1800–1955*, p. 33.

51. Cohn, *op. cit.* (1962), pp. 312–320 *passim;* A. M. Shah, "Political System in Eighteenth Century Gujarat," *Enquiry*, I (1964), 88.

c) Regional: This level of political organization consisted of appointees having a localized jurisdiction who
owed their positions to the imperial or secondary authority. They were often autonomous, and only loosely tied to
national power.

d) Local: The local political level comprised lineages,
tax officials, adventurers, and indigenous chiefs.[52]

Although Cohn's distinction between "imperial," "secondary," and "regional" political levels is essential to an
understanding of traditional government hierarchy, these
levels did not influence equally the local situation. From
the point of view of a Rajput stratified lineage, the imperial and secondary levels of authority were distant, often
unknown, in an interactional sense. Because the impact
of a state (whether imperial or secondary) was mainly felt
through its regional appointees, I have condensed the
first three of Cohn's levels into an undifferentiated "central authority" or "state power."

In the larger theoretical sense, however, these studies indicate that coercive power and civil jurisdiction were
greatly dispersed in traditional North Indian polities.
Just as the distribution process gave many different groups
access to the cultivator's grain heap, so too the political
institutions allowed many different levels and personages
a share in decision-making and political management.

Cohn neatly summarizes the situation:

In pre-modern societies, although some individual, family,
or group may be conceded absolute authority within the
political system, power and authority most frequently are
distributed among vertically or hierarchically ordered groups.
. . . No one group or individual, because of the nature of
the value system, the economy, technology, and the social
structure, can dispense completely with other groups. . . .
Consensus and balance are achieved through conflict and

52. Cohn, *op. cit.* (1962), p. 313.

through the awareness that there are always other groups ready to step in. The systems to which I am referring seem to be perpetually on the verge of breaking apart.[53]

Aidan Southall's model of the "segmentary state" seems applicable to the North Indian situation. Southall's criteria are:

1) Territorial sovereignty is recognized but limited and essentially relative, forming a series of zones in which authority is most absolute near the centre and increasingly restricted towards the periphery, often shading off into a ritual hegemony.

2) There is centralized government, yet there are also numerous peripheral foci of administration over which the centre exercises only a limited control.

3) There is a specialized administrative staff at the centre, but it is repeated on a reduced scale at all the peripheral foci of administration.

4) Monopoly over the use of force is successfully claimed to a limited extent and within a limited range by the central authority, but legitimate force of a more restricted order inheres at all the peripheral foci.

5) Several levels of subordinate foci may be distinguishable, organized pyramidally in relation to the central authority. The central and peripheral authorities reflect the same model, the latter being reduced images of the former. Similar powers are repeated at each level with a decreasing range.

6) The more peripheral a subordinate authority is the more chance it has to change its allegiance from one power pyramid to another. Segmentary states are thus flexible and fluctuating.[54]

States in North India with these qualities can be viewed as segmentary in two ways: First, their power is segmented

53. *Ibid.*
54. Aidan Southall, *Alur Society*, pp. 248–249.

so that the central authority does not have primary responsiblity for many local political decisions; second, the local political institutions which do bear such responsibility are based on a segmentary lineage system.[55]

A segmentary state by nature compartmentalizes political activity into discreet social segments which strike a balance of strength and weakness. When the pendulum of power swings from the local segment to the center or vice versa, it induces a changed relationship between them. Such power shifts also alter the internal constitution of both.

In a segmentary state, the role of hinge figures or institutions is extremely important. Such roles balance the segment and the state authority. Often these intermediaries are partly of the center and partly of the local political segment. The lineage elite had such an intermediary role in a political as well as a revenue sense between the central power and the kin brotherhood.

55. The latter point is implicit in Southall's treatment of Alur segmentary states in East Central Africa, even though it does not appear in his general definition. I note it here because the review of state development in chapter four accentuates the importance of segmentary kin groups encapsulated in bureaucratic or feudal polities. In a later publication, however, Southall suggests that a segmentary state need not only be based on segmentary lineages. Indeed, the latter is a special case according to Southall's more recent view. For the purposes of this presentation, and in consideration of the comparative materials presented in chapter four, a definition of the segmentary state which includes the presence of a lineage or unilineal kin principle is warranted. However, compare Southall, "A Critique of the Typology of States and Political Systems," *Political Systems and the Distribution of Power*, pp. 126ff.

3

THE DEVELOPMENTAL CYCLE
OF THE RAJPUT LINEAGE

T HE BRIEF description of kinship, the raja, and the state in the previous chapter is highly generalized. It intentionally avoids problems of land tenure, powers of the lineage elite, republican and autocratic lineages, and spurious and real rajas or talukdars. Unresolved arguments over these matters run through the British settlement reports of the nineteenth century. The conflicting theories arise from the failure to see Rajput lineages and their political functions as evolving institutions which take different forms and perform different functions at different times. For example, one enduring argument concerned the local men of influence called talukdars in the revenue records. Were they hereditary lineage leaders or were they merely state-appointed tax farmers? A middle position stated that some were "true" lineage heads with delegated revenue functions and others were "spurious," who held their positions at the discretion of central authority or had seized it during a period of anarchy.[1] Underlying all these opinions is the belief that talukdars or lineage heads were chosen once and for all in the past. It makes a false distinction between the older and accepted lineage heads as "pure," and upstarts who had not yet consolidated their position or ramified their kin groups as "impure." The British ignored the fact that their process of genesis was similar, and that they performed equivalent functions within their kin groups. The British revenue authorities simply assumed that age proved the social role. In assigning proprietary rights, which was the major problem confronting the early British revenue officers, length of time in power was a distinguishing criterion between rightful land holders and usurpers. However, the revenue authorities also believed they were distinguishing social categories of importance to native society in their classifications.

The distinction between *pattidari* and *bhaiacharya* land tenures also confused the British. In pattidari tenures a group of kinsmen paid the government revenue and divided up their directly cultivated lands on the basis of ancestral shares. Land held in bhaiacharya tenure was distributed on a nonancestral share basis—often in an egalitarian fashion according to family size and need, which required periodic redistribution. Some British commentators sharply distinguished these two tenure patterns, and speculated on the tribal origins of the bhaiacharya, while ascribing the pattidari system to state land grants given to court notables.[2] In fact, the bhaiacharya and pattidari

---

1. For a discussion of these positions, see Millett, *Settlement of the Sultanpur District,* para. 139–143.

2. See Baden-Powell, *Land Systems of British India* I, 109; II, 131. Barden-Powell believed that many bhaiacharya tenures also originally arose from nonjoint village communities in which cultivators individually owned and worked their fields. Their corporateness he

tenure systems appear to be on two opposite ends of a
continuum of tenurial development in northern India.[3]
What British revenue administration succeeded in doing
was freezing social segments of the local society at one
point in time. The colonial government then took the
resulting snapshot of the social hierarchy as indicative of
discrete social groups and categories which had existed in
the same relative positions throughout the history of
North India.

British observations concerning proprietary title and
revenue engagement are not sufficient as a description of
North Indian local political organization. To understand
the dynamics of political life in preindustrial northern
India, and the give and take of power between different
levels of political organization, we must dispense with the
synchronic, typological approach toward the Rajput lineage. The following pages describe the Rajput lineage in
terms of a developmental cycle. Studies of family structure
have used this concept to go beyond the misleading synchronic typologies of "joint," or "nuclear," or "matrifo-
cal." A developmental approach to the family supposes
that different stages in the cycle of domestic history have
differing forms of familial organization.[4] Similarly, a
cyclic view of the Rajput lineage allows variation in the

believed to be an artifact of the British land-revenue policy in the
Northwest, which treated all villages as if they had a corporate
brotherhood of proprietors.

3. Cf. Bernard Cohn, in Robert Eric Frykenberg, ed., "Structural
Change in Indian Rural Society," *Land Control And Social
Structure in Indian History*, p. 104. I came across Dr. Cohn's sug-
gestion of a developmental cycle in North Indian tenures after
completion of this chapter. It is good to know that another scholar
has arrived independently at similar conclusions.

4. Cf. Jack Goody, ed., *The Developmental Cycle in Domestic
Groups*. For a discussion of the developmental cycle approach in
political anthropology, see Mark J. Swartz, Victor W. Turner, and
Arthur Tuden eds., *Political Anthropology*, p. 3.

structure of specific lineages at different times. It describes the process of lineage development and the factors which lead one lineage to be at a developmental stage different from another. This approach also allows us to observe how radically different forms of kinship, chiefship, and state influence may characterize different points in a lineage's developmental cycle.

Some of the early British civil servants recognized the value of a cyclic or developmental viewpoint. A. F. Millett, for example, attempted to explain the varying conditions which resulted in the development of either an auto-cratically governed "clan" or a highly ramified and seg-mented "peasant proprietary." [5] Millett also wrote of the development of bhaiacharya villages and how they differed from those held in pattidari tenure.[6] He seems to have shared the views of Robert G. Currie who noted in 1874 that the British takeover of Shahjahanpur district had stereotyped land tenures at one point in their evolution from pattidari tenures into bhaiacharya tenures.[7] In the next pages, I attempt to follow out the leads of these Brit-ish revenue officers, and more fully describe the develop-mental course of the Rajput lineage.

A caveat is necessary concerning the fit between de-velopmental cycle and temporal succession. The scheme presented below is not chronological. The course of his-torical events and lineage organization differed from one locality to another. Within a limited region, lineages in different stages of development might be found. At the time of the British occupation of the Uttar Pradesh re-gion, lineage identification and political organization were increasing as a result of the anarchy induced by Mahratta

5. A. F. Millett, *Report of the Settlement of the Land Revenue of Fyzabad District* (1880), para. 187. (1873), para. 151.

6. Millett, *op. cit.*

7. Benett, *Report on the Family History of the Chief Clans of Roy Bareilly District*, para. 75.

incursions. However, in each successive British revenue settlement the powers of the lineage leaders became increasingly eclipsed, until, in the Agra and Benares provinces, they were completely set aside.[8] A similar attempt to abolish superior revenue rights in Oudh contributed to the outbreak of the Mutiny of 1857.[9] The British suppression of superior proprietary rights was in keeping with the traditional actions of strong central governments in northern India. The difference was that the British state developed an enduring economic and military power base superior to native polities. The latter permitted British hegemony to endure and solidify beyond what was common for traditional North Indian states.

FACTORS IN THE DEVELOPMENTAL CYCLE

The developmental cycle of Rajput lineages has four interrelated factors. Some of these concern the ecological and demographic dispositon of the lineage. Others concern its relationship with the central authorities. The factors are:

1. The amount of land available for territorial expansion. Territorial expansion consisted either of bringing

8. For example, in Moorsan pargana of the Aligarh district, the raja of Moorsan was allowed to engage to pay the land revenue on the entire pargana during the early British revenue settlements. After 1824, the year of the raja's death, his descendants were set aside by the British, and the estate was settled with village headmen or with tax farmers without any inquiry having been made into the proprietary titles. See Anonymous (M. P. Carnegy), "The Talookdaree Tenure of Upper India," *Calcutta Review*, XLIII (1866), 137–160. Other examples of the state politics behind revenue settlements are given in Richard G. Fox, "The British Settlement of the Northwestern Provinces" (unpublished manuscript, 1962).

9. See Thomas Metcalf, "From Raja to Landlord: The Oudh Talukdars, 1850–70" in Frykenberg, ed., *Land Control and Social Structure in Indian History*, pp. 125–126.

waste or underpopulated lands under cultivation or physical conquest of populous cultivated regions. Virgin tracts existed in the *terai* region bordering the Himalayas in the time period under discussion. Waste lands arose due to famine, epidemics, or wars when cultivators left their lands or were decimated. Outright conquest depended largely on the population and prowess of the lineage. Territorial frontier conditions greatly influenced the internal organization of Rajput lineages and were an indication of their relationship with the central power. In general, territorial frontiers existed only when the state was weak because anarchic periods created waste lands, and the state, when powerful, could militarily restrict or control lineage expansion.

2. The population, cohesiveness, and military success of the lineage. These factors are often closely related. A large population usually aided military prowess in the initial stages of a lineage's development or when the central power was weak. However, a large population often caused the kin body to be less cohesive and corporate. Since kin cooperation was necessary for military success, population and cohesion were balanced—or else the lineage fissioned. The cohesiveness which underlay the military force of a kin group was sometimes based on kinship etiquette and genealogical appeal. Later cohesion was the result of the internal stratification of the lineage which gave the raja and elite a predominant authority. Similarly, military cooperation at first emerges mainly from kinship discipline; later on, it is due to the "feudalization" of military service owed the lineage elite.

3. The nature and power of the lineage elite. This factor is closely tied to the level of stratification within the lineage. Sometimes, internal rank and economic differentiation within a lineage was small. When this occurred, the minimal lineage of the hereditary or elected

lineage leader (if such a role was defined) was no more elevated than other minimal lineages of the kin brotherhood. The lineage leadership merely represented the interests of the lineage as a whole, and its bargaining ability with central authority depended on the military threat of the entire kin body.[10] At other times, stratification within the lineage was great, and the lineage raja and his close kinsman formed a power group which often seized the proprietorship and other prerogatives of their kinsmen. In such lineages internal hostility ran high—the disenfranchized lineage members rebelled, and palace revolts occurred in the lineage elite. Whether or not a raja proved powerful depended in some measure on his charismatic definition of his office. But, more important, it depended on the favorable concurrence of the factors of population, military success, territorial expansion, and the organization of the state.

4. The nature and power of the state. When the influence of the state at the local level was weak, the state had little power to control local events or counter a strong lineage, except perhaps by internal subversion. When strong, the state might decide to subsidize newcomers to reduce a turbulent lineage and its elite to cultivators. Or the state could undertake military punishment of dissident lineages. The kin segmentation or military success of a lineage was often greatly influenced by the actions of central authority. If the state were powerful, it could restrict the expansion of a lineage even though waste lands or natural frontier existed. A strong state hindered the internal stratification of the lineage which therefore did not develop a raja to embody and enforce kin corporateness. Lineage fragmentation was the result. Thus the state was not merely passive in the face of local developments. It actively subsidized elements of the local

10. Cohn, *op. cit.*, pp. 107–111.

order which it favored and subverted those which it opposed.

State strength was primarily evidenced in a local area through state-appointed governors and revenue contractors. The royal court entered little into the routine management of the domain, and often permitted its representatives extensive police and military powers over large regions. The personal qualities of such governors, their individual wealth, court contacts, and military following determined how successfully they represented state authority. Their official tenures or contracts were of short duration. Nevertheless, a powerful and wealthy governor might impress strong state authority on a region where previously state control had been nominal. A weak and inexperienced government appointee might dissipate state influence. Great distinctions in political conditions might arise between adjacent regions subject to different governors.[11] As a result, variations in lineage cycles sometimes occur independent of the power of the royal court or the political norm for the region during a specific time period.

These four factors are not presented as a complete causal recipe for the development of lineages. Clearly, not all four factors are equally independent variables. Nor does this essay provide any method of independently meas-

11. Sleeman relates the history of a community of Kanpuria Rajputs in the Salone district (Oudh), and their relationship to changing state-appointed governors. From 1827–1836, Dursun Singh a powerful man, controlled the district and kept the Kanpurias subdued. He cut down many of the jungle tracts where they took refuge to escape payment of state revenue. A subsequent governor continued and even extended central control over this Kanpuria lineage. In 1848, however, a weak and inexperienced central appointee was given the district, and within a few years the Kanpurias had reasserted themselves. By the time Sleeman visited, they had restored all the former jungle, strengthened their forts, and regained the lands they had lost. Sleeman, *A Journey through the Kingdom of Oudh in 1849–1850,* I, 241.

uring the importance of these factors. In the following pages, when I note that, for example, a certain form of lineage organization occurs if the state is weak, I have no independent measure of state weakness other than the several or multiple historical concurrences of state weakness and this form of Rajput organization. This comparative methodology which I employ to show functional correlation may not satisfy those who wish to know *why* the state was weak. At the present stage of my materials and competence, I am unable to answer such questions. This study only attempts to note the stages of Rajput lineage development and some of the changing combinations of variables associated with the stages. It defines which areas of social interaction and behavior seem significant for understanding lineage growth and decline. This procedure is tautological. Tautologies, however, are useful in examining interrelated factors which hitherto had gone unseen and in promoting further research.

The developmental cycle below presents the evolution of structural forms in a single kin group. Yet, at any period, a general regional uniformity of lineage structure existed because of the significant role played in the Rajput cycle by state power. When the state was weak, local reaction created a uniformity in lineage structure. When the state was strong, it could enforce homogeneity of lineage organization. At any period, however, pockets of nonconformity existed—open rebellion, local disobedience, corrupted state officials tolerant of lineage power, or especially strong lineage personalities who could reverse the direction of the times. The relative relationship of local kin groups to the state authorities in any generation was a complex melange of developmental stages, of varying degrees of state power, and of fluctuating territorial acquisition. If the following presentation overemphasizes the uniformity or discreetness of the developmental stages of a lineage, it must be remembered that my goal is not an exegesis of the temporal record. My goal is, rather, to illuminate the structural principles of lineage organization and to suggest the causal factors behind lineage development.

The major criterion of lineage structural development used below is the number of intermediary groups between cultivator and central authority. When the number of such intermediary groups changes, significant structural alteration occurs in the lineage, and it passes from one stage to another. On the basis of this criterion, five major stages can be distinguished in the developmental cycle of a Rajput lineage. Not every lineage passed through *all* developmental stages. Some were permanently fixed due to adverse circumstances. Others bypassed some stages. The duration of each stage differed from one lineage to another.

STAGE ONE

BIRTH OF THE LINEAGE

Political upheavals at the time of the Muslim conquest of northwestern India are often cited as the cause of Rajput migration to the eastern Gangetic plain. Many Rajput myths also trace their origin to a founder, in flight from the idol-smashing Muslim conquerors. However, some British revenue authorities believed in an age of tribal migration between the eleventh and thirteenth centuries.[12] The British suggest a preliterate society of Rajputs in migration wherein thousands of Rajputs left home and country. This picture seems difficult to reconcile with the limitations of contemporary transportation and communication facilities. Early amateur ethnographers often

12. Cf. Baden-Powell, *The Indian Village Community*, pp. 121–128.

posited improbable migrations to explain changes in social customs—a penchant based on their fallacious equation of race and culture. They were unable to understand
social change except in terms of population displacements.
More probably, Muslim-induced political dislocation affected the elite ranks of the Rajputs and their followers—
at least those who survived—since these groups posed the
greatest threat to foreign domination. The great tribal
movements into Uttar Pradesh which appear in Rajput
oral legend and British accounts may, in fact, only have
been scattered bands of disenfranchised and disinherited
Rajputs, intent upon visiting their fate on others. Other
evidence suggests, however, that such migrants did not
arrive unheralded, but rather at the behest of state powers
or even in the train of the Muslim conquerors.

The two variants of the origin myth of the Bachgotis
illustrate this matter. In one version, Barriar Singh Chauhan is said to have fled his ancestral home to seek asylum
from the Muslims who had singled out the Chauhans for
ill treatment. He settled in the Sultanpur district (Oudh)
about A.D. 1248 from where his descendants migrated to
form new colonies and make new conquests. The other
version has Barriar Singh and his twenty-one brothers dispossessed by their father in favor of the son of the latter's
second wife. Barriar Singh seeks his fortune in the en-
tourage of the Muslim, Alla-ud-Din Ghori, who is on his
way from Delhi to subjugate the Bhars (the supposed
authochthones of much of eastern Uttar Pradesh). Part
of the conquered Bhar country, the original Bachgoti
patrimony, is given to Barriar in return for his services
to the Muslim state.[13]

13. Neville, *Sultanpur: A Gazetteer*, pp. 78–79; Millett, *op. cit.*
(1873), para. 281–290. Baden-Powell, *op. cit.* (1896), p. 128 concludes that most Rajput migrations were small-scale and limited to
dispossessed individuals and their followers.

What seems to have characterized the founders of Uttar Pradesh Rajput lineages was their political and military pioneering on the margins of state political authority. Whether they were the agents of encroaching Muslim imperialism or refugees from the latter's devastation, these lineage ancestors brought under control tracts of land outside the orbit of central state authority. At this time the traditional leadership was weak or nonexistent in advance of Muslim conquest. The social categories that took advantage of such political opportunities may have already been in the area or they may have been the fleeing remnants of indigenous authorities, now reduced to banditry or perhaps state-recognized privateering. I take this period as the base point of the Rajput developmental cycle.

Stage one of the lineage cycle sees the state as weak or absent, and lineage ancestors-adventurers arising and spreading relatively unhindered to stake their claims to local political power. Sometimes the lineage founder settled on virgin land. At other times he reclaimed waste areas uninhabited or underpopulated due to disease and war. In virgin or waste territory the lineage ancestor often acted as an agricultural entrepreneur. By grant of various preferments, he invited tenants to begin cultivation. In populated areas, the lineage ancestor through cunning and force of arms reduced pre-Rajput inhabitants to simple cultivators or forced them to flee. Such conquests often resulted from territorial bequests made by state authorities or regional strong men to adventurers. These grants were usually lands on the margins of the state authority, and over which it exercised, at best, nominal control. The adventurer had to validate the patent of the central authorities with his own courage and strength.

Stage one of the Rajput cycle is therefore characterized by only one intermediary between the cultivator and the state—the lineage ancestor and his close agnates plus whatever mercenary or non-kin military personnel he might employ. The state was weak, and land revenue flowed directly to the lineage ancestor and his kin associates. Because the lineage founder had only just established his preeminence, his kin group had not branched out. His few agnatic kinsmen were closely bound to him in their enterprise of conquest and rule. The lineage ancestor collected payments from the cultivator or from a village headmen, with whom he had no kin relationship (although the cultivators may have been organized into village coparcenary bodies).

The virgin *terai* region of Gonda district (which Bennett described) was occupied at this stage of lineage development. Benett carefully shows that the roles of raja and "clanship" are unrelated.[14] He notes several Gonda rajadoms in which the ruling "clan" consisted of a single family which did not belong to the clan of its agricultural subordinates. What Benett saw as proof of the lack of fit between political power and kinship organization must be seen in the light of a developmental cycle. The lands had recently been opened up, the rajas had just come to power, and therefore the ruling lineage had not yet proliferated. The Gonda rajas of the *terai* region represent the lineage founders of stage one. At this stage kinship is not an important principle in organizing local government because the significant kin bodies are hardly more than minimal lineages.

As the lineage ancestor's control over a territory increased and his lineage ramified, a more complex situation arose. At first, emergent cadet lines were provided for by permanent assignments of some of the main agnatic lines' villages. But since the state remained weak, and conditions anarchic, the possibilities of territorial expan-

14. Benett, *Report of the Final Settlement of the Gonda District*, para. 65.

sion through military might or guile were great, and cadet lines moved to new areas to try their fortunes. For example, within three generations the Tenwa Jats spread over an area of eighteen talukas which comprised the tappa of Joar.[15] In a matter of generations the Bachgotis spread throughout the Sultanpur, Faizabad, and Pratabgarh districts and into a segment of Jaunpur.[16] Map 6 attempts to portray the dispersal of the Bachgotis over several generations.

The take-over technique used by Rajputs seems to consist of equal measures of force and slyness. Sleeman provides a vivid picture of the conquering Rajput in action. A Brahman told him how the Rajputs

get land little by little at lease, soon refuse to pay rent, declare the lands to be their own, collect bad characters for plunder, join the Rajpoots of their own clan in all the villages around in their enterprises, take to the jungles in the first occasion of a dispute, attack, plunder, and burn the village, murder us and our families, and soon get the estate for themselves, on their own terms from the local authorities, who are wearied out by the loss of revenue arising from their deprivations.[17]

This case is taken from a period of state decline after a time of strength (similar to stage four (*a*) described below). Except for the state's recognition of the *de facto* local situation, however, it could stand as a picture of Rajput expansion in stage one.

The immigration of cadets was undoubtedly subsidized by the lineage members in the main line of descent who

15. John Thornton, "Report Upon the Settlement of Pergunnah Moorsan, Zilla Allygurh," reprinted in Hutchinson, *Allyghur Statistics, Being a Report on the General Administration of that District from A.D. 1803 to the Present Time.*

16. See Millett, *op. cit.* (1873), para. 281–311.

17. Sleeman, *op. cit.*, II, 57.

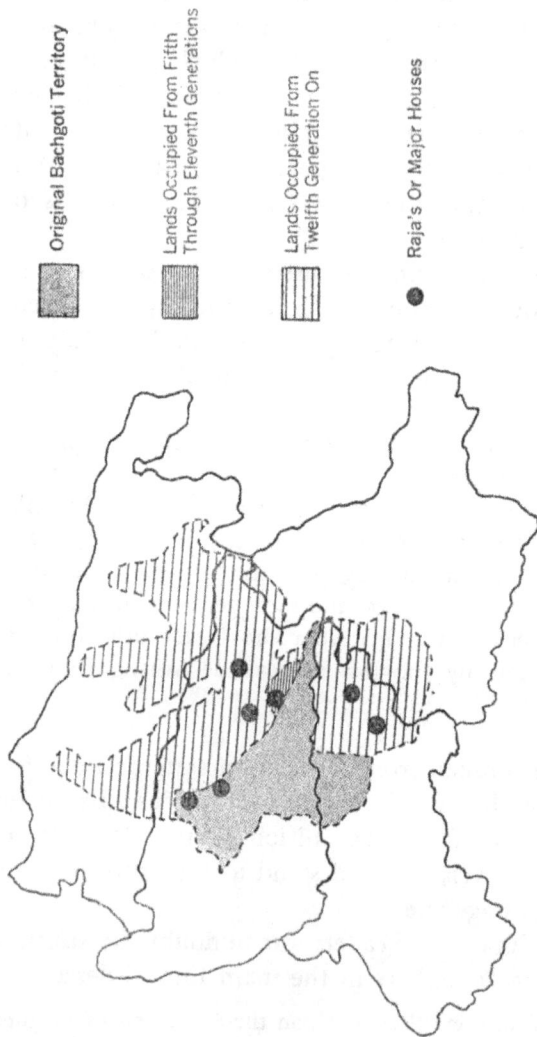

Original Bachgoti Territory

Lands Occupied From Fifth
Through Eleventh Generations

Lands Occupied From
Twelfth Generation On

● Raja's Or Major Houses

MAP 6. Territorial Dispersion of the Bachgoti Category. The development of lineage rajas or important houses occurs at the frontiers of the lineage territory, and seems related to territorial expansion and addition to the lineage territory.

did not wish potential competitors any nearer than necessary. However, the main line ancestors had little to protect at this stage. Although status distinctions begin to emerge between senior and cadet lines, the distinction was more concerned with kin etiquette than economic or power differences. Land was available and inferior kin lines did not need to accept inferiority in wealth. Benett reports that when a raja's estate (*rajya*) was divided in Gonda, the younger branch took the position of junior members in a confederation, and were later either reabsorbed or became independent. He notes that when Muslim power was strongest, most fissioning occurred, whereas when the central authority was weakest, the Hindu chiefdoms formed the most powerful confederations.[18] A similar opinion is voiced by Millett concerning the Faizabad district:

> Where the clan settled without a struggle, and where the partitions occurred in more recent times when a more perfect civilization and a firmer Government had removed in part the tendencies to combination under a patriarchal system, the detachments which parted from the main body habitually asserted independence as a proprietary community.
>
> These I believe were the principle conditions which determined the growth of the original property into a steadily expanding taluka, or diverted it into a succession of peasant proprietors constantly subdivided.[19]

Throughout this first stage, then, the internal organization of the kin body was directly related to ecological pressures and population increase, rather than to external political pressures. Because of the territorial frontier and the inability of the weak state to restrict movement, the

18. W. C. Benett, *A Report on the Family History of the Chief Clans of the Roy Bareilly District*, para. 67.

19. Millett, *op. cit.* (1880), para. 186.

lineage of the founding ancestor quickly dispersed over a wide area. As a consequence, a great deal of kin fissioning occurred. When the lineage reached a certain level of complexity and geographical spread, it broke into two separate stratified lineages, to some extent tied by sentiment and common heritage into a "confederacy." This continuous fragmentation and dispersion prevented complex stratification within each lineage. In later stages kin fissioning is primarily motivated by political considerations, rather than territorial dispersion and genealogical complexity.

If, in stage one of the Rajput developmental cycle the state is weak, a loose confederacy of Rajput stratified lineages, each inhabiting its own territory evolves. These lineages are genealogically shallow and internally egalitarian because close familial ties outweigh status and wealth considerations. Each lineage consists of a founder and his close agnates who collect produce and rent directly from the villages under their control.

If the lineage evolves under strong state authority (as Millett discusses above) the rate of fissioning is accelerated, the chiefs and descendants in the main agnatic lines are less influential, and an increasingly fragmented and republican lineage proprietorship results. Such a situation might arise when the anarchy which attracted adventurers is only temporary or local, or when the lineage ancestor is only one step ahead of state control. Lineages which are forced into this path through overweening state control were often characterized by large numbers of coparceners within proprietary units. These lineages also often held their lands in bhaiacharya tenures, were fragmented and ramified, and belonged to stages three and four of the developmental cycle. Their characteristics are discussed below. I turn now to the developmental path taken by those lineages which evolved under conditions of weak central authority.

STAGE TWO

RISE OF THE RAJA

Stage two in the developmental cycle of the Rajput lineage occurs when internal stratification increases and when a large body of agnatic kinsmen develop. In this stage, two economic and political classes come between the central authority and the cultivator: the powerful and autocratic lineage elite, usually identified with the lineage raja, and the large body of his subordinate and often oppressed kinsmen, often identified as village zamindars.

Two developments seem to trigger the second phase of the cycle:

1. The state begins to mitigate the anarchic conditions which characterize stage one and therefore starts to encroach on the autonomy of the local lineage confederations. This encroachment usually takes the form of a demand for revenue. This situation seems to develop in areas where the central power has military strength, but cannot or will not establish complete civil authority. Although subdued, the area remains a marginal and indirectly managed segment in the preindustrial state. The revenue demands of the central government are lodged with the leaders or kin elite of each stage one lineage proprietary group because the state is relatively weak in the region or has limited political goals, and because local lineage sovereignty has just recently been breached.

This use of existing corporate institutions by the state for revenue payment reflects the weakness of central authority during stage two. Early in their settlement of the Northwestern Provinces, the British realized that they could gather more revenue by dealing with the cultivators or village-level "proprietors" than by going through revenue intermediaries. However, several decades passed before they could institute all of the machinery, assemble all of the records, and gather all the staff to institute a direct system of collections. Belligerent local elites also impeded their efforts.[20] The native states which used the raja and his elite kinsmen as revenue payees did so because they had no administrative or military alternative in the early years of their occupation of a conquered tract.

Lineage leadership before this time was primarily determined by genealogy and was unimportant to internal economic stratification or political coercion. Although this imposition of revenue demands by the state clearly restricted the autonomy of the lineage leadership, it also served to elevate them with respect to cadet lines of their own lineage. When the state assumed authority over revenue collection, the close-knit family-based lineages of stage one (within a confederacy) individually began to develop into the impersonal, "feudal" kin bodies that comprise the most common literary stereotype of Rajput clans. The imposition of revenue demands by the state curtailed genealogical fission, and served as a punitive weapon with which the lineage leadership commanded conformity and allegiance. The revenue demands served as a vehicle for those in power to take over lands illegally from their lower-status, weak, and distant agnates. In short, revenue policy helped create the role of lineage raja and elevated him over his subordinate kinsmen. Such an elevation in status occurred even when the raja resisted state authority. A raja might refuse to pay state revenue demands, yet would exploit local fear of central authority to increase his power. Although the raja and elite might threaten the state with the military potential of the kin-based legions, they increasingly use state authority to replace such ties of kin affect with those of feudal domi-

20. Refer to the case of Thakur Dya Ram of Hattrass in note 45 of chapter two.

nance. Eventually, the extended genealogy of the lineage serves only as the merest gloss of etiquette over a relationship between elite and followers, between prince and poor.

Several early British revenue authorities understood this relationship between state revenue mandate and strong lineage elite. To give the full text of the quote from Oldham cited earlier:

> The Mahomedan Government, except during the period when the revenue policy of Akber and of his minister Todur Mull was in force, recognizing the unity of the Rajpoot tribes, often made the Rajah or chief responsible for the land revenue of the whole tract in the occupation of his clan; and thus by the recognition of a supremacy already existing, helped to enforce and perpetuate it. The Rajah, while the sole proprietor of only a few villages, yet had to realize and discharge the land revenue of all the villages in the pergunnah; and in this manner, in process of time, acquired a kind of superior proprietary right in the whole tract.[21]

Benett in his history of Rae Bareilly clans reports much the same process. He notes that when Saadat Khan invaded Oudh he was faced with the problem of uniting the hostile countryside. To effect this, he acknowledged the rule of the lineage chiefs in their parganas and settled the revenue collection with them. Benett writes, "The arrangement was in every way a good one, as the pargannah boundaries very generally corresponded with the limits of the chieftain's authority and the distribution of his clan, and each was already furnished with a body of hereditary revenue officials." [22] Under the Muslim settlement in Oudh, a chieftain payed no rent on his own villages and continued to collect customary "tribute" from

21. Wilton Oldham, *Historical and Statistical Account of the Ghazeepoor District,* part I, p. 43.
22. Benett, *op. cit.* (1870), para. 82.

his kin following. He was also free to allocate uncultivated lands among his followers and dependents. But the chieftain could no longer assign the revenue of an entire village to one of his cadet relatives, which illustrates his loss of autonomy to the central authority: ". . . his position is forcibly illustrated by the permission occasionally given him to purchase the right of engaging for the government demand as proprietor in particular villages in which he already collected the revenue as head of the pargannah." [23] Benett emphasizes the weakening of the lineage leadership by their incorporation into the revenue machinery of the central government. However, like Oldham, he clearly perceived that this economic institution which weakened the lineage leadership at the national level, greatly strengthened it in dealings with the lineage following at the local level.

In his report on the British settlement of Gonda, Benett provides greater detail on the factors which brought about increasing stratification within the Rajput lineage, although he did not perceive these developments as influencing kin bodies. Benett sees the Gonda situation described in stage one as typical and original—a raja or leader collects land revenue directly from cultivators to whom he is not related. This condition may be perverted by the introduction of money and the encroachment of external state power on the raja. The introduction of money leads many rajas to farm out their share of the land revenue to individuals who guarantee them a money payment and meet the revenue demands of the superior state power. Therefore, recourse to this method of revenue collection is intimately tied to the weakening of the local rajas' powers, attendant upon foreign conquest and dom-

23. *Ibid.*

ination. According to Benett, such original revenue farmers have evolved into village proprietary bodies; the villag zamindars of the present.[24] This theory is in keeping with Benett's deemphasis of kinship as a positive factor in state-local relations, and his belief that all talukdari tenures originally arose from simple rights to revenue farming.[25] His position is an extreme one, and not in keeping with the fact that in general local lineage heads alienated their rights in village productivity to cadet lines of their own kin group. Benett's analysis, however, is important because it points out the role of external state control in creating a new, subordinate group of village-level zamindars who stand between the cultivator and the lineage elite.

But why do such cadet lines need to be provided for in stage two, if they present no problem in stage one? This question is answered by the second major determinant of the passage from the first to the second stage of the lineage developmental cycle. Internal economic and political stratification within the Rajput lineages increases in stage two because of the unavailability of a territorial frontier into which to disperse cadet lines. The disappearance of the frontier is not solely an ecological matter, but is more determined by social groups occupying the land. The literature indicates that the frontier ceased to exist when the Rajput lineages in stage one had dispersed and fully occupied all lands which were waste, virgin, or could easily be taken from the indigenous inhabitants. As the Rajput lineages came increasingly into direct contact with each other geographically, the old military and organizational techniques which had proved sufficient in the conquest of the aboriginal populations, virgin forests, and lands thrown out of cultivation, were no longer enough to in-

24. Benett, *op. cit.* (1878), para. 84–88.
25. *Ibid.*, para. 94.

sure success against other Rajputs of equal military stature. At this point the office and personage of the lineage raja and the basis of the power and wealth of the lineage elite become established.

Baden-Powell believes that clan rajas arose in times when the necessity for joint protection of the kin body led to the election of a superior leader who was honored with the title of "raja" by the central power.[26] Millett in his Sultanpur report notes that not all talukas had a *gaddi* or chiefship, and consequently not all talukas were characterized by impartibility, a trait which was congruent only with a *rajya* estate. He believes, however, that in times of stress, impartibility and seemingly, therefore, a gaddi or rajadom might occur in all talukas.[27] The Bisen

26. Baden-Powell, *op. cit.* (1892), II, 133.
27. Millett, *op. cit.* (1873), para. 143. Further corroboration is offered by Lyall's studies of the independent Rajput kingdoms of Rajasthan. Although differing in internal political dynamics because of the absence of a superior territorial state, the Rajput polities nevertheless reflected internal conditions similar to those found among their "brethren" of Uttar Pradesh. For instance, Lyall comments on the rise of powerful lineage rajas in time of stress: "In the Eastern Rajput States, which were most exposed to the disintegrating ravages of the Moghal and Maratha, the tribal organization has been much effaced politically, and the Chief has centralized his power and acquired almost complete jurisdiction over the whole of his territory. So that whereas in the North and West a ruling Chief could not break through the compact front which his clansmen would at once oppose to any serious political encroachment, and has a dubious jurisdiction within the domains of his leading kinsmen, in the South a Chief rules a State more or less under his own administrative orders, and a population of which his own clansman form but a small part." Lyall's last sentence will be pertinent to my discussion of the results of lineage conquests for internal lineage and external political relations. In conclusion, Lyall offers the general statement: "Where the clan organization is strongest and most coherent the Chief's dominion is smallest, and largest where the Chief is, or has lately been, a strong, energetic and therefore acquisitive ruler." Alfred Lyall, *Asiatic Studies, Religious and Social*, pp. 216, 208.

Rajputs of Gonda, Gorukhpur, Faizabad, and Pratabgarh districts created such a lineage raja where no preexistent office of lineage superiority had existed. During Akbar's period, all Oudh Bisens were ordinary village zamindars, "dividing their inheritance among all the males on the ordinary coparcenary principle," but in later times, a "few fortunate houses" acquired the title and position of raja both in the extreme north and south.[28]

Primogenitural succession and proprietary impartibility are important diagnostics of the rise of the raja. They provide both a superior genealogical base and a proprietary position upon which the office of a powerful lineage leader might rest. These institutions do not characterize Rajput lineages in stage one. The appearance of these institutions in stage two is congruent with the creation of strong lineage rajas. Sometimes, primogeniture and impartibility are judged as independent, causal variables. In this view, strong rajas existed where such jural rules held sway; where absent, a kin "republicanism" existed. The following discussion treats primogeniture and impartibility as adaptive responses to changing social conditions rather than as jural or ideological givens. To understand their development, the nature of inheritance rules relative to evolving social forms must be traced. The question becomes: Why is primogeniture present or absent during a particular period? How does this fact reflect the larger social milieu of the times?

Unfortunately, no adequate explanation of the origins and growth of primogeniture and impartibility exists in Indian literature. Instead the analysis below depends upon the European (mainly Irish) development of these institutions described by Sir Henry Sumner Maine.

Maine noted that the origin of primogeniture was "one of the most difficult problems of historical jurisprudence."

28. Benett, *op. cit.* (1878), para. 33.

He found that primogeniture appeared late in the Teutonic world, after the Romans had crossed the Rhine. The early form of primogeniture differs from its later development. Sometimes, it was not the eldest son who inherited the office of chief. Rather, the eldest male relative succeeded, and sometimes the succession had to be ratified by the assembled kinsmen.[29] For example, the custom was thus described in the 16th century:

> It is a custom among all the Irish that presently after the death of any of their chief lords or captains, they do presently assemble . . . to choose another in his stead, where they do nominate and elect for the most part, not the eldest son, nor any of the children of the lord deceased, but the next to him of blood that is eldest and worthiest, as commonly the next brother if he have any, or the next cousin, and so forth. . . . They do appoint the eldest of the kin to have the [chiefship], for that commonly he is a man of stronger years and better experience to maintain the inheritance and to defend the country.[30]

With this historical background, Maine argues that primogenitural succession arises from the breakdown of ancient, tribal methods of succession to chiefship. He posits that inheritance of high tribal offices originally passed through a single minimal lineage which was considered superior in descent to all others. No specific individual from this lineage was by birth destined to be chief, rather the entire tribal body invested the office on one particularly able individual from the leading lineage through election.[31]

In Europe, primogenitural succession eventually re-

---

29. Henry Sumner Maine, *Lectures on the Early History of Institutions*, p. 199.

30. Quoted from Spenser's, *View of the State of Ireland*, in Maine, *op. cit.*, p. 201.

31. *Ibid.*, pp. 201–202.

placed the older method of chief selection. The lands attached to the office of tribal chief also came to be passed down in primogenitural fashion. Gradually, nonpartible inheritance became established for all lands held by the chief—including those which he controlled as an appurtenance of his office and those he owned as a private person. Later this pattern became the established law of succession for all elite groups in feudal Europe.[32]

Although material on the history of Indian succession customs is poor, the little at hand does not differ markedly from Maine's exposition. Primogeniture develops in Rajput groups which were formerly characterized by partible inheritance and election of tribal representatives (see quote from Millett above). Sleeman found that among rajas and talukdars who succeeded in primogenitural fashion, estates were considered principalities (*reasut*). Cadets were assigned parts of the reasut for their maintenance. This act effectively removed these lands from the principality and caused them thereafter to be equally partitioned in each generation among the cadets according to the normal rules of inheritance.[33] A raja could decide, however, to disregard the rule of primogeniture and divide equally his lands among his sons. The history of any Rajput group contains many instances of such events.[34]

Moreland notes that conquered Rajput chiefs under Mughal domination still maintained a pattern of nonpartible inheritance. He concludes that

This practice points to a recognized distinction between 'property' which under the developed Sacred law is ordinarily divided at death, and 'chief right' which is not divided, and must be regarded rather as a survival of sovereignty.[35]

32. *Ibid.*, p. 204.
33. Sleeman, *op. cit.*, I, 172.
34. See Baden-Powell, *op. cit.* (1896), p. 306.
35. William H. Moreland, *The Agrarian System of Moslim India*, p. 174.

Primogeniture and impartible inheritance in Europe
and India thus develop quite separately from the common
laws of succession. "Primogeniture is not a natural out-
growth of the family [in its widest sense]. It is a political,
not a tribal institution, and comes to us not from the
clansmen, but from the chief." [36]

If primogeniture and impartibility are indeed political
institutions, then politics must provide the reasons for,
and process of, its development. Maine equates the rise of
primogenitural practices with internal and external conditions that permitted or necessitated an increasingly
powerful executive authority within the tribe. He specifically mentions the maintenance of peace over long
periods of time and the development of military and civil
institutions grouped around the central authority of a
chief or ruler.[37] The cooptation of the Rajput lineage
elite into the revenue machinery of the North Indian
state is certainly an instance of the development of centralized institutions around a chief. This, perhaps, is one
reason for the growth of autocratic rajas with primogenitural succession and impartible inheritances. A second
reason—the managerial abilities of a powerful leader and
his organization of a more defensible kin domain—is
discussed below.

The raja appears to function in time of stress as a political institution when he copes with the increasing com-
plexities of lineage success and the management of lineage
expansion. This organizational activity of the raja coupled
with his subsidization by the state revenue machinery
seem to have strengthened the main agnatic line of lineage
leadership found in stage one into the often autocratic
and powerful kin rulers of stage two.

The correlation between lineage success in territorial
acquisitions and the presence of a raja confirms the asser-

36. Maine, *op. cit.*, p. 223.
37. *Ibid.*, p. 202.

tion above. Lineages which were hemmed in by more powerful lineage neighbors or which suffered from internal kin and proprietary fragmentation did not have powerful rajas or elites. Evidence for this position is not great, partly because many British revenue authorities assumed that the office of raja was a natural institution hardly requiring comment or explanation. Nevertheless, the most famous lineages and rajas were generally recent immigrants to a region who were forced to push older, established Rajput kin groups out of their path. Powerful elites developed on the margins of their territory where they were actively engaged in competition with other lineages. In the Faizabad district, the Rajkumar Bachgotis were the last lineage to enter, but they quickly outstripped and dispossessed the formerly powerful kin brotherhoods of the Sakawars and Raghbanshis. The latter groups had in turn earlier gained supremacy over various lines of Brahmans and Kurmis.[38] Faizabad is a center of particularly strong lineage leadership among the Rajkumars, which probably explains their ability to subdue other once powerful lineages. Map 6 indicates the territorial dispersion of the Bachgotis, and shows how powerful houses developed only on the expanding borders of the original lineage territory. To be successful, a latecomer lineage had to possess an organizational advantage over the incumbent kin groups: this advantage seems to have been provided by increasingly powerful lineage elites.

Lack of a lineage raja accompanied internal fragmentation, inability to expand into new territories, or absorption by other lineages. Such a fate befell the relatively powerless Bachgotis in the pargana of Asal (Sultanpur). They had no idea of primogeniture or kin raja, and have fallen into obscurity. Their villages were the most mi-

---

38. Millett, *op. cit.* (1880), para. 359.

nutely divided of all in the district.[39] Much of their misfortune probably results from their geographical situation: they were an enclave, hemmed in on all sides by more powerful Bachgotis to whom they were related but whose success in territorial conquest and whose internal social stratification they did not share. The history of the Gaur Rajput taluka in Powayn pargana of Sultanpur is also instructive. Originally, the Katheria Rajputs controlled this tract. They were later pressured by aggressive Muslim groups moving out of the newly settled city of Sultanpur. The Katherias were unable to resist effectively these incursions because they had been weakened by the partitioning of several cadet families. Central authority within the lineage to organize resistance to the Muslims was

39. Millett, *op. cit.* (1873), para. 311. Lyall also indicates that in those independent Rajput communities of Rajasthan which did not develop primogeniture, no powerful central direction of the kin group emerged. He gives the example of the Mullanee Rajput "sept" which has no chief of its own. "It is made up of a number of distinct family groups, each separate and independent under its head. And the land is not only parcelled off among these groups, but there goes on a constant struggle between the ordinary rule of Hindu succession to property, which divides off the land among the sons at each succession, and the rule of political expediency which inclines toward primogeniture. The ordinary outcome of this struggle is a sort of inchoate primogeniture, allotting a larger portion of the family lands and superior authority to the elder heir of the chief family in a group. But the blood feuds, family and faction fights, and general anarchy caused by these chronic quarrels over the land are incessant, and have totally prevented any political consolidation of the sept into a State." Lyall also describes the condition of the Kuchwaha Rajput "clan." "This consists of the descendants of a son of an ancient Chief . . . who went forth and conquered this tract on his own score and private venture. They have never formed a State under one tribal leader, and they still continue in the molecular condition of an uncertain federation of family groups of different magnitude, usually dividing and subdividing the land down to the point consistent with some kind of cohesion for self-protection and the recognition of a head to each family." Lyall, *op. cit.,* pp. 217–218.

lacking. When the Katheria raja was killed in battle, his
wife, a Gaur Rajput, enlisted the aid of her kinsmen. The
latter proved more successful in resisting the Muslims,
and eventually the entire pargana fell under Gaur Rajput
control completely supplanting the leaderless Katherias.[40]

A younger branch of the ill-fated Katherias had settled
across the Gumti river in a heavy jungle infested with
malaria. There no partitions threatened the integrity of
the lineage, and the raja was the sole guarantor of his
relatives and lands. The Gaur Rajputs did not succeed in
taking over this tract.[41]

Undoubtedly many factors determined why a specific
lineage would be too weak to dispel its aggressive neighbors, and end up subordinate to them. Lack of numbers
and the active opposition of state authority could count
as heavily as fragmentation or weak leadership. My material is not sufficiently detailed for a more definite resolution. Lineages which were circumscribed by powerful
neighbors underwent the same developmental process as
those which endured control by powerful state authorities (as described for lineages of stage one and for stages
three and four (*b*) below.) They were both characterized
by great proprietary fragmentation and an abundance of
lands directly cultivated by the kin brethren rather than
being given out to tenants. In stage two however, these
developments were caused by the local power situation,
and such weak lineages therefore often fell prey to conquest by more powerful neighboring lineages.

The impact of conquest on internal lineage organization and stratification is discussed below. However,
two alternatives to total conquest existed which had less
drastic repercussions on the balance of power in a local

40. Robert G. Currie, *Report on the Settlement of the Shahjehanpore District,* p. 111.
41. *Ibid.,* p. 108.

area. A lineage might be so weak that it could not defend peripheral territories which it had wrested at an earlier date from an incumbent lineage. When this happened, it merely yielded the gains of its own earlier aggression on neighbor kin groups rather than losing its political and economic independence entirely. Another alternative for a weak lineage was to ally with a powerful kin raja who would guarantee its integrity. This solution was often only a temporary expedient which did not fundamentally alter the position of the weak lineage. Dharamir, a Bandhalgoti Rajput of the Sultanpur district, received as a patrimony an estate of forty-two villages. He became the ally of Raja Hasan Khan, the famous Khanzada (Bachgoti) leader, and was rewarded with five other villages. This estate was quickly reduced in influence by partitions, and by its inferior position—hemmed in on either side by the territory of neighbors whom they could not defeat.[42]

The conquest of one lineage's territory by another is common in stage two. Unlike stage one, the conquering lineage brethren do not generally settle the new territory. Rather, the conquering lineage elite asserts a preeminent position over these new lands, and becomes the major link with central authority. In stage two, military conquest is an appurtenance of the lineage raja, and the spoils of conquest go to him and his close agnates. In the example of the loss of the Katheria Rajput tract to the Gaur lineage, the property went to the family of the Gaur Raja rather than being distributed among his entire lineage.[43] The conquered lineage is left in possession of its lands and, at the village level, of much of its managerial discretion over cultivation. However, the families

42. Millett, *op. cit.* (1873), para. 332.
43. Currie, *op. cit.*, p. 111.

of preeminence in the conquered lineage are reduced to the status of their fellow kinsmen.

Often such conquered territories became the patrimony of a specific son or close agnate of the conquering raja. Thus the situation commonly arises that a foreign raja and his close family reign over a lineage with which he has no kin tie. Such instances have sometimes been taken as anomalies which disprove the role of kinship in North Indian political organization. The complexity of the situation, however, must be kept in mind. A stratified lineage could function in two different organizational frameworks at the same time. A raja who ruled a territory inhabited by nonkinsmen possessed (or had possessed) as well a power base in a lineage locale composed of his own kin brethren. Over time, the conquering raja's family or that of his appointee would proliferate, and what at one point seemed only a small family set atop a large subservient lineage body (with which it had no connection) might become an internally stratified lineage of great depth in its own right. In such instances, the conquered lineage would increasingly be reduced in wealth and property until its members were indistinguishable from common cultivators.

Access to external wealth and land through conquest greatly buoyed the powers of a lineage raja and his elite. A raja was constrained by kin ties and potential mutiny from an overharsh governance of his own lineage territory. Nothing, however, prevented him from economically or politically exploiting the lands which fell to him by conquest. Sleeman found that although local elites in Oudh cultivated their hereditary possessions well, those lands which they acquired through fraud or violence were poorly managed.[44] The objective was to strip the land and its former proprietors of all wealth and produce, not to

44. Sleeman, *op. cit.*, I, 56.

nurture them. Undoubtedly many dispossessed proprietors became tied to the conquering raja as bodyguards or non-kin militias. Both the land and people provided the lineage raja with an exploitable source of wealth and personal following independent of kin etiquette and obligation, which magnified his economic superiority and patrimonial power over his kin brethren.

The external political functions of the lineage elite and their military conquests had important consequences for internal lineage organization. In stage one and the succeeding stages discussed below, kin allegiance outweighs class and power distinctions within the lineage. However, in stage two, internal stratification greatly diminishes the importance of kin connection. Kin ties are still important to the military organization of the lineage, the division of inheritance, and the selection of the lineage leaders. Apart from these, however, burgeoning internal stratification leads increasingly to loss or re-interpretation of kin obligations in terms of power class differences. In stage two, the raja is more raja than kinsman.

As the descendants of the original settlers proliferate and military conquest of easily accessible lands becomes more difficult, the cadet lines of the stratified lineage become a major problem. Absence of readily available frontiers mandates the rise of the raja, and provides him with a subservient body of kinsmen. Space in the original lineage fort-settlement decreases, and junior kinsmen are provided with maintenance grants in nearby villages that form part of the common patrimony. Potential contenders for lineage positions are no longer dispersed from the seat of lineage influence as in stage one. Cadet lines are also likely to prove troublesome because of the decreased possibility of achieving an independent rajadom elsewhere.

Over a few generations cadet lines quickly decrease in status and wealth, or else successfully usurp the position of the lineage elite. Their inferior position and physical proximity increasingly made them the vassals of the lineage elite. Each succeeding generation of cadets was forced to partition equally their original, limited subsistence grant. At this point, many inferior lineage brethren were forced to take up direct cultivation on at least part of their ancestral lands. This land, called *sir* in the revenue literature, is an indication of increase in lineage population within a limited territory, and by extension, a reflection of the growing inferiority of large segments of the kin body. The larger the proportion of sir, the more the body of lineage brethren had been reduced to cultivators, and the more they were subordinate to the lineage elite or an outside authority.

The increasing stratification within the lineage usually created strains between the raja and his cadet lines or even more distant kinsmen. During stage two, the lineage elite emerge as a definite, segmented economic and political class with interests different from, or at odds with, those of their lineage mates. The raja begins to play the role of intermediary between state and lineage without belonging fully to either camp. He acts as savior to his kinsmen because he can protect them from oppressive state revenue exactions; but he is also a threat to them because of his control over state proprietary policies. He acts as a savior to the state because he can extract revenue from his dissident kinsmen; but he is also a threat if he decides to harness this pugnacity in a local revolt.

The raja and his minimal lineage often attempt to convert the state mandate for revenue collection into a proprietary or managerial right. They try to dispossess their distant kinsmen, the village zamindars, from managerial or preferential control over lands other than their directly cultivated sir. If successful, the lineage elite reduced their brethren to undertenants or cultivators. Many times, this development is promoted by a weak state, as for instance when central authority dispenses with all revenue officials and farms out revenue collection to the highest bidder. Under such conditions, the raja and lineage elite were often called upon to protect their kinsmen from the unprincipled and rapacious demands of the tax farmers: "And so the old talukdars, or the heads of clans aggregated to themselves vast additions of territory, for the clansmen put in their hands the engagements for their villages in hopes of an escape from excessive taxation." [45] This quotation refers to a period of weakness in state organization which followed a time of great central authority. The developmental cycle as I have discussed it here is a continuous evolution of increasing state involvement in local affairs beginning with a weak and politically removed central authority. However, lineage rajas undoubtedly infringed upon the proprietary rights of their village kinsmen whenever a weak state's revenue coercion or rapacity became great and the protection offered by superior status and wealth became necessary.

The village zamindars did not automatically lose all proprietary or managerial functions when absorbed into the directly-administered holdings of the lineage elite. What proprietary upheavals, in fact, transpired depended greatly on the relative strengths of the lineage elite and their village kinsmen in the local area. Millett suggests four potential arrangements: 1. The elite might succeed in completely ousting the village proprietors from all superior rights and reduce them to occupancy tenants. Such a development seems to reflect a level of internal lineage stratification in which the elite belonged in little more than name to the same social group as their now-

45. Millett, *op. cit.* (1880), para. 188.

dispossessed village relatives. 2. The elite left the village zamindars in possession of their directly cultivated lands, but assumed the management and possession of the rest of the estate. This arrangement was less destructive to the village proprietors than the first alternative. 3. The elite might only be able to gain control over the waste and jungle lands of the village proprietors. 4. The elite were not able to alter the managerial and proprietary rights of their village-level kinsmen in any fashion.[46] In the latter two alternatives the separation in power and status between the elite and the lineage following was not great. Sometimes an arrangement for convenience and protection between a raja and his village kinsmen developed into a highly exploitative situation. In general, large estates based on shared kinship enjoyed liberal relations between the village zamindars and their proprietary overlords.[47] The village zamindars at times even believed they could withdraw from the estate and pay their revenue directly to the government or join another large estate.[48]

However, what the village zamindars thought they could do and what they actually could do in opposition to their lineage elite were different matters. As the power of the elite increased, they found new methods of coercion outside their kin legions to threaten the state, and to keep their increasingly subordinate kinsmen in hand. They brought in private bodyguards to help protect them from government revenue authorities or their own kinsmen. Sometimes these bodyguards were the impoverished sons of lineage brethren who sought their fortune in service rather than on an inadequate patrimony. Here, clearly, the bonds of distant kinship with the elite are subordi-

---

46. *Ibid.*, para. 189.
47. *Ibid.*, para. 234.
48. *Ibid.*, para. 218.

nated to the political power and paternalism of the lineage raja. At other times, such bodyguards belonged to other lineages, perhaps to those weaker or conquered kin bodies which aligned themselves with a powerful rising elite. Such bodyguards at times usurped the power of the lineage leaders. When lineage mates overthrew a raja, such palace revolts led to a different reigning lineage dynasty. If the bodyguards were outsiders, a whole new lineage superior to the former employer's might arise. The latter development brought into being a tenurial situation similar to the conquest of a lineage by a foreign raja. The lineage elite compensated these bodyguards with gifts of land acquired through the elite-managed territorial conquests characteristic of stage two. (See the example of the Bandhalgoti Rajputs, above.)

The village zamindars had several means of resisting the incursions of their own lineage leaders, short of direct military confrontation. In periods of great pressure from central revenue collectors, the village-level kinsmen could choose to "mortgage" their property holdings to individuals or groups with whom they had no kin affiliation. These individuals might include the rajas and elites of other lineages, Brahmans and other ritual authorities, or even moneylenders.[49]

Working behind the back of their own lineage elite was an intentional risk taken by the village zamindars in the interest of maintaining their own autonomy. This development tends to skew the fit between proprietary or revenue paying unit and kin body by introducing foreign elements into lineages, and by involving nonkin superiors in revenue payment. A similar development results from the conquest of a lineage by a foreign raja. From this point on, and especially in succeeding stages when the state is strong, a growing inconsistency and discontinuity between kin borders and the boundaries of revenue or govern-

49. *Ibid.*, para. 183.

mental territories evolves. Increased state control or increased stratification at the local level through the emergence of lineage elites lessens kinship as an organizing principle of political and revenue constituencies in the local area. This evolution continued under British colonial administration until the modern system developed in which administrative divisions bear no relationship to former lineage territories.

A final way in which the lineage elite might try to subordinate their *distant* kin was through grants to cadet lines of lands over which the elite had only nominal control or none at all.[50] Such grants entitled the cadets to collect the revenue in villages already occupied by distant members of the lineage, the descendants of older cadet lines, who had sunk to an undistinguished status. If the grantee-cadets could oust their distant brothers, they gained control over what had been given them in patrimony by their lineage elite. Such developments again demonstrate the subordination of kin organization and sentiment to economic stratification and political power.

In addition to distant kinsmen, the lineage elite in stage two must deal with the cadet lines of their own lineage. In general, interaction between lineage elite and cadets is another facet of interaction with the state. Because the state is relatively weak, its main influence on local political action seems to have been to reward those in power with honorary titles and sumptuary perquisites. As an alternative the central authority subsidized the claims of one elite faction against the other, and thus disrupted or at least influenced the power balance within the lineage.[51] Throughout the interaction of the lineage elite with their cadet lines, therefore, one sees the state

50. Millett (1873), para. 179.
51. Many examples of such Machiavellian practices appear in the literature. See the discussion of the Khanzada and Kurwar talukdars in Neville, *Sultanpur: A Gazetteer*, pp. 88ff.

as an important element in determining the course of events.

An example of the state's recognition of local power concerns Nundram, a Tenwa Jat who lived at the time of Aurangzeb (1658–1707). Nundram became so powerful at the local level that when Aurangzeb ascended the throne, he conferred upon him revenue management of the entire tappas of Joar and Tochghur, and also allowed him police powers over the district. Nundram's family remained influential in the local area even after British accession. For a long time they enjoyed complete possession of the zamindari of the region, and also continued to retain control over the police. Not until 1816 did the central authority—the British East India Company—feel sure enough of its might to subdue successfully this Tenwa Jat family on its home grounds.[52]

A cadet line might, however, attempt to employ recognition by the state to separate from, or usurp, the powers of the main lineage raja and elite. In general, a cadet kinsman of the raja was granted some rent-free villages for his subsistence in the first generation of proprietary separation. In subsequent generations, if the *babu* or leader of the cadet line was an enterprising personality, he often managed to get a separate revenue engagement with the government. (This entailed a revenue settlement with the lineage of minimal incorporation.)[53] Such separate revenue recognition by the central power appears to have served as a springboard from which to launch an independent cadet line. Just as often, however, the main line of lineage leadership proved stronger than the cadets, and the latter

52. Hutchinson, *op. cit.*, pp. 17–18.
53. I. F. Macandrew in Millett, *op. cit.* (1880), para. 9. Millett, *ibid.*, para. 178–179, believed that the central power coerced cadet lines into paying a separate revenue, a practice tolerated by the lineage raja because it weakened the cadet line.

could not achieve a separate revenue settlement. In succeeding generations, the lineage elite often placed a low rent on the originally rent-free villages. Over time, this impost increased until the kinsmen who held these villages were reduced to the economic subordination of the other distant kin.[54]

Stage two of the Rajput developmental cycle leads to the concentration of economic and political power in the hands of a lineage raja and elite increasingly removed from the local kin base and local concerns which originally gave them influence. Stage three is a continuation of this process in which nonlocal power groups control the nature of political organization at the local level.

STAGE THREE

INTRUSION OF THE STATE

Stage three of the Rajput developmental cycle is characterized by two developments which appear to contradict each other. First, new elites at the local level are formed as a direct result of state intervention in local affairs. Second, the old lineage elites are rendered powerless and reduced to the status of their kin followers. As a further anomaly, the new elites created by the state were at times staffed by the old lineage leaders, who had grown so removed from their old kin base that they operated as independent adventurers at the local level.

The power of the state binds these developments together. Both the destruction of the preeminence of the former lineage and the creation of new leadership is undertaken by the state in stage three and indicates its increased control over local politics.

Benett recognized the role of the state in the evolution

54. Macandrew, *op. cit.* (1880), para. 9.

of the Rajput lineage into stage two and subsequently, stage three:

> Under the vigorous administration of Akbar and his successors, the Hindu clans were naturally much depressed, and driven . . . nearer the soil. Their connection with the villages in their domain became much closer, new villages were founded, and the increasing number of each family led to the establishment of the non-cultivating village proprietors who are known in our courts as old zamindars. The intervention of a foreign rule and the diminished danger of invasion from without, deprived the Rajas of half their attributes, the principle of unity was lost sight of, and each member of a leading house was able when he separated to assume in his new home almost all the privileges retained by the head of his family. The ties of kinsmanship were however still vividly recognized. At the end of this period instead of a few unconnected Rajas, we find hierarchies of powerful zamindars, each immediate proprietor and landlord of a few villages from which he drew his subsistence.[55]

Benett attributes much of the state's influence over local kin groups to increased kin fissioning brought on by state guarantees of protection. Undoubtedly, increased kin segmentation in times of state strength did lessen status preeminence and economic stratification within the lineage. However, the state attempted to destroy the lineage raja and elite as intermediaries between it and the body of the lineage in more direct ways.

Perhaps the most important manner in which the state intruded on local political organization was in the assignment of the right to collect the government land revenue. Baden-Powell noted that "the revenue history of Oudh before annexation largely consists . . . of alternations between attempts of the state to collect the revenues direct,

55. Benett, *op. cit.* (1870), para. 74.

and having recourse to collection through Rajas and others under the denomination of Taluqdars." [56] When the state was strong, it could afford to replace the intermediaries which stood between it and the village-level proprietors. Therefore, when central authority at the local level was great, the lineage elites were at first set aside with an allowance, and then eventually reduced to the same level as their kinsmen, the village zamindars. In stage three only the village zamindars stand between the central power and the cultivator. This situation remains true until the central government chooses to relinquish its rights to local land revenue in order to form a new, dependent local elite.

Balwant Singh, a powerful raja of Banaras, provides a good example of the extermination of the lineage elite through state fiscal policy. Under East India Company policy instituted in 1795, the raja of Banaras was empowered to decide questions of revenue within his family domains. The British did not recognize subsidiary tenures, and only permitted the raja to bring complaints before the commissioner.[57] From this point on, the raja began to extinguish all rights which stood between him and the cultivator. Like Akbar, he attempted to destroy the power of the pargana zamindars who in large measure were the old lineage rajas and elite. Later he attacked the proprietary and managerial powers of the village zamindars.[58] In place of the pargana zamindars, the Banaras raja appointed subordinate revenue officers who answered directly to him and who were often related to him by kin ties.[59]

56. Baden-Powell, *op. cit.* (1892), II, 206.
57. W. Duthoit, "On Ryot Right in the Family Domains of the Raja of Benares," in W. Muir, *Notes on Tenant Right, On Right to Subsettlement, and On Rights of Jagheerdars,* p. 101.
58. W. Muir, *op. cit.,* p. 75.
59. Oldham, *op. cit.,* part II, pp. 44, 93.

Other strong rulers also adopted this direct system of revenue collection. Although the early rulers of Oudh appointed lineage rajas to collect revenue from the lands of their kinsmen, later potentates abandoned this practice.[60] The lineage elites were greatly distressed at becoming the pensioners of the state, and made their displeasure known forcibly to the central power (see below).

The sentiment of strong state authority in northern India seems faithfully mirrored in the following quotation:

For the smaller the engagements, and the less considerable the landholders, the more we secure the interior peace of the country and a ready obedience to Government . . . all which ends are obstructed by great and turbulent landholders, who in this part of the country appear, for the most part, to have become so by nothing else than usurpation over their brethern.[61]

This statement was not made by a native Indian ruler, but by Jonathan Duncan, a British revenue officer and resident in Banaras. It is not surprising that the British adopted a revenue policy similar to the one followed by strong Indian states. What guaranteed the political stability of a region for a raja or navab would do the same for His Britannic Majesty's company. Throughout the early years of company rule in the Northwestern Provinces, the government often at first employed a local raja for revenue collection but later reversed itself and set him aside.[62] The realities of military and political power rather than philosophical or fiscal policies caused this change. As soon as the British felt their position secure enough to oppose locally powerful revenue intermediaries, they began to set them aside.

What is the status of the lineage elite of stage two who

60. Benett, *op. cit.* (1870), para. 84.
61. Oldham, *op. cit.*, part II, p. 147.
62. See note 45 of chapter two.

have come under the control of a powerful state? The central authority began to eliminate them by making revenue collections directly and paying the hereditary leaders a percentage of the receipts (*nankar*). The amount of nankar varied with the strength of the local proprietor.[63] Eventually the government felt strong enough to circumvent the hereditary elite completely and the allowance would be stopped. (Such was the procedure of the East India Company in the Northwestern Provinces.) The lineage elite still controlled the lands they held in direct management, but without their political influence as revenue intermediaries their position and stature shrank until they were indistinguishable from their lineage brothers except, perhaps, in formal title. Predictably, the hereditary lineage leadership resisted this development. Early British civil servants in the Northwest observed that the greatest bandits or *dacoits* came from the better classes.[64] Elite dacoits were especially prevalent in Oudh where the rulers exacted exorbitant revenues with British indulgence in the latter days of their rule. These dacoits were dispossessed lineage elites whose only recourse was local guerilla resistance and robbery.

Sleeman wrote of the large proprietors of the Sundeela district (Oudh), that:

The Government officers are afraid to measure their lands, or to make any inquiries on the estates into their value, lest they should turn robbers and plunder the country.[65]

As state intervention in local affairs increases during stage three, lineage elites retreat to localities which offer sanctuary from government oppression. Such refuge areas tend to be at the borders of state systems—lands which are

63. Sleeman, *op. cit.*, II, 24.
64. Benett, *op. cit.* (1870), para. 85.
65. Sleeman, *op. cit.*, II, 1.

politically marginal, and topographically *jangli* or wild.[66]
In India jangli refers as much to territory which was
uncultivated due to lack of political protection as to non-
arable country. An African-inspired image of such jungles
would be incorrect. They were often quite small (for
example, nine miles in length by four miles in width);
incongruous havens in the midst of otherwise highly cultivated fields.[67] Some jungles were the result of the intentional planting of bamboo and other thick growing spe-
cies by lineage elites wishing to protect their forts. In
other situations, lineage elites carefully maintained the
extant jungle.[68] Whenever the state became sufficiently
powerful, it introduced great local clearing projects to
throttle the political wilderness and cut down the dense
floral cover.

Lands which had the greatest chance of remaining
politically "uncultivated," even in times of maximum
state strength, lay at the no man's intersections of empires
or at internal backwaters of a realm. The British territories of Uttar Pradesh were in this condition shortly
before the annexation of Oudh. Bandits pillaged in Oudh,
and retreated to the bordering British districts to escape
prosecution. Such marginal country existed in all periods.
From such favored locations, the dispossessed lineage
elite who had turned bandit carried on constant guerilla
warfare against the politically stable agricultural regions.

One old man graphically portrayed the problem to
Sleeman:

After the East India Company had, by good government,
made us all happy and prosperous and proud to display the
wealth we had acquired on our persons, and in our houses

66. *Ibid.,* p. 95.
67. *Ibid.,* p. 231.
68. *Ibid.,* pp. 279ff.

and villages, you withdrew all your troops . . . and left us prey to the wild barons of the hills and jungles on our borders, whose families had risen to wealth, distinction, and large landed possessions under former misrule and disorder, and who are always longing for the return of such disorders, that they may have some chance of recovering the consequence and influence which they have lost under a settled and strong Government.[69]

Such elite outlaws had the choice of either continuing local guerilla actions against the state, hoping the state would weaken or relent, or they might assemble their armed followers and migrate to a new territory where state power was minimal. If the state did indeed weaken, the dispossessed lineage elite along with the bandits might repossess some or all of their former revenue estates. This situation, which actually occurred at the end of native rule in Oudh, is described in stage four (*a*). If the disposed elites migrated to a new territory, such armed parties entered into a new developmental cycle: they represent the lineage ancestor-adventurers described in stage one above. (See stage five below for a description of this reintegration of the developmental cycle.)

Because the lineage rajas and elites were diminished, the lineage brethren benefited relative to the harsh conditions of stage two. The government settled the revenue demand with the village zamindars, usually the village headmen or representatives of minor lineages called *mukaddams*. In chapter two, I indicated that this level of government revenue incorporation should not be viewed as the smallest lineage segment recognized corporately by the state. The reason for this statement is now clear. In a strict kinship sense, the minor lineage headed by a mukaddam was indeed the smallest corporate kin body

69. *Ibid.*, p. 95.

recognized by the state. But viewed in terms of the political functions of the Rajput lineage, the state recognition of the mukaddams was tantamount to denying the lineage any local political viability. Such recognition meant that the state had successfully circumvented and impoverished all preeminence at the local level above the village-based, relatively powerless minor lineages of the Rajputs.

The new elite emerges in stage three not as the result of military prowess, but of state revenue appointment. Officials, court favorites, military officers, and others were often granted government revenue collection rights over a specific tract. State power was transmitted to the local area through these personages. Usually, such lands were already occupied by Rajput lineages who either fought to retain their managerial rights or who were forced to accept the new revenue intermediary.[70] Although the old lineages fought hard, their demise was hastened by the weakened condition of their hereditary elites, similar to the conquest of a lineage area by a foreign raja in stage two. The power of the revenue appointee, however, is delegated from a strong central authority, rather than being dependent on a lineage territorial base.

The state appointees provided the mechanism for setting aside and eliminating lineage rajas and elites. Contemporary British sources referred to the "absorption" of estates by higher authorities—the removal of local lineage elites and the transfer of their holdings to government appointees and court favorites. In this absorption, the government officers attained a dual identity: they were agents of the central authority, yet their proprietary role at the local level placed them in a new category of rural elite. The objective of the royal court was to contain its appointees' powers while still using them to eliminate

70. See Cohn, *op. cit.*, pp. 97–99 on Lakhnesar pargana and the Sengur Rajputs.

strong lineage leaders. The object of the appointee was to transform his delegated court position into a sounder one based on local property, influence, and wealth.

Sleeman's description of the governor, Dursun Singh, indicates the use to which the Court put such appointees:

> Dursung [*sic*] Sing was strong both in troops and court favor, and he systematically plundered and kept down the great landholders throughout the districts under his charge, but protected the cultivators and even the smaller land proprietors, whose estates could not be conveniently added to his own. When the Court found the barons in any district grow refractory, under weak governors, they gave the contract to Dursun Sing, the only officer who could plunder and reduce them to order.[71]

Dursun Singh's rise to power exemplified the rise of new local elites through state subsidy. He began life as a trooper in a company of light cavalry, an appointment he gained through his father's influence as a minor bureaucrat. In 1817 Dursun Singh was given five villages in *jaghir* (nonproprietary revenue management) because of his services to Saadat Khan, ruler of Oudh. By 1820, Dursun Singh had gained full proprietary title to all these lands through rackrenting, mortgage, and other fraudulent or violent means. By 1827 he had successfully pursued the same system in other parts of the country which passed under his control and held lands which yielded rents of 590,000 rupees annually. He later devised a plan for forcibly extracting deeds of sale from the proprietors of lands he had seized in order to legalize his acquisitions. Dursun Singh and his brother were the most extortionate, feared, and effective governors during the declining days of the rulers of Oudh.[72]

Over several generations, the appointee's personal line-

71. Sleeman, *op. cit.*, I, 58.
72. *Ibid.*, I, 151–152.

age proliferated, and eventually a large body of local co-sharers developed, which in many senses duplicated the kin bodies of the long resident Rajputs. In time, a powerful, main agnatic line might begin to segment from a larger body of cadet inheritors. If this evolution continued unabated, various lines were forced to take up cultivation directly, and sir land-holding developed. As the appointee lineage ramified, and land requirements increased, they squeezed the lineage exproprietors more vigorously until the latter's managerial rights were completely extinguished.[73]

Because the state was strong, the appointee lineages of stage three were artificially restricted in their ability to expand through territorial conquest. Such kin units were also generally too small to present a challenge to the state. Therefore, the state-appointee lineages could not rely on their kinsmen for military assistance. Instead, they depended on favoritism by the court. The state restriction on territorial expansion also encouraged kin corporateness in such lineages, and restricted fragmentation. Since power was delegated to the lineage from a central source, cadets had to remain close to the main agnatic line or rapidly fall into obscurity. Stage three cohesiveness should be compared to stage one lineage fragmentation which occurred when the state was strong and local lineages were in power. In both cases, however, the state discourages the growth of independent, locally autonomous lineage rajas such as those of stage two.

Not all of the new appointee elite stemmed from individuals foreign to an area. The literature indicates that the state often chose its appointees from local men who were on the way up, and whom the state hoped to win into its administration before they could engineer a revolt. Many of these new men were the old lineage rajas and

73. Cf. Sleeman, *op. cit.*, II, 88 and I, 153.

elites. When such local men were appointed, stage three
had progressed to the point where the lineage elite stood
completely separated from their lineage brethren by economic and political stratification. State strength only
meant that these local aristocrats were absorbed as *individuals* (rather than as representatives of their larger
lineages) into the governmental machinery. Thereafter
their descendants might form a separate lineage, superior
in wealth and power to their former local relatives. This
development is best illustrated by the Khanzada Bachgotis
of eastern Oudh. Sometime during the Mughal period,
Tilok Chand, a Bachgoti descendant of Barriar Singh
Chauhan, was favored by the Muslim court and earned
the honorary title of "Khan Bahadur." He converted to
Islam and took the name of Tatar Khan. The major part
of his inheritance passed to two sons of his second wife
who were raised as Muslims. This line became known as
Khanzadas and rose to great prominence in eastern
Oudh.[74] Although structurally it is not of the same genealogical depth as the other Bachgoti lines, the Khanzadas
are given a separate status equivalent to the Rajwars,
Bachgotis, and Rajkumars (see chart one).

Another example is the Gautam Rajput of Tappa Sow-
lulabad in the Azamgarh district, who at the end of the
sixteenth century found his patrimony insufficient and
set off in search of fortune. He joined the imperial court
at Delhi, rose to favor, and gained control over twenty-
two parganas, including much of present-day Azamgarh.
From 1609–1771 the family controlled this tract, and its
head became known as the raja of Azamgarh.[75]

Many British revenue authorities of the nineteenth

---

74. Millett, *op. cit.* (1873), para. 292; also Neville, *op. cit.*, p. 88.
75. Thomason, *Report of the Collector of Azimgurh on the Settlement of the Ceded Portion of the District Commonly Called Chuklah Azimgurh*, p. 9.

century viewed appointee lineages of stage three as impure because they owed their rise to recognition by the state, they were of more recent origins and hence smaller than lineages of ancient "freebooting" origins, and because the rights of occupancy tenants (the former village proprietors) were more obvious.[76] I now turn to stage four of the Rajput cycle—the stage the British found in Oudh at the time of its annexation, and the rather different condition of the Northwestern Provinces at the beginning of British hegemony.

STAGE FOUR

Stage four of the Rajput lineage developmental cycle is characterized by two different structural possibilities. If the state's intervention in local affairs suddenly weakens from the high levels of stage three, the resultant anarchy leads to new strength in the lineage leadership and the promotion of the independence of the appointee kin bodies. If, however, central authority continues to control local events to the same degree as in stage three, Rajput lineages are further reduced in stature. Eventually not only are the elites set aside, but the village-level kin body is threatened.

(a) RENAISSANCE OF THE RAJA

The rajas and the lineage elite were reestablishing themselves at the time of the British annexation of Oudh in 1856. For reasons which need not concern us here, this principality was in political turmoil, and local conditions bordered on anarchy. Rule of might was the only guarantee of property and life. In many areas the Lucknow rulers had farmed land revenue collection to the highest

76. See Millett, *op. cit.* (1873), para. 139.

bidder, and the result was a reign of local terror and economic exactions enforced at swordpoint.

The local response to the pillage and terror and the weakness of the central authorities was a return to former ways of protection. Millett reports that the old "clan" heads, set aside under the vigorous administration of the early rulers, regained strength, and their village kinsmen turned over the engagements for their villages to them in the hopes of escaping the excessive taxation.[77] Benett reports that the lineage system reasserted itself as a result of the anarchy in Oudh during the Mahratta wars. He stresses the protective role of the lineage raja, and his ability to organize the kin body into an effective military force with which to resist central power.[78]

The weakness of the central authorities during this period allowed the formerly dispossessed lineage elite to recoup some or much of the properties which they had controlled in stage two.

Sleeman vividly describes the growing anarchy in Oudh after 1814:

As the local officers of the Oude government became weak . . . the talookdars became stronger and stronger. They withheld more and more of the revenue due to Government, and expended the money in building forts and strongholds, casting or purchasing cannon, and maintaining large armed bands of followers. All that they withheld from the public treasury was laid out in providing the means for resisting the officers of Government, and in time, it became a point of honor to pay nothing to the sovereign without first fighting his officers.[79]

Millett and Benett indicate that at times the village zamindars-kinsmen cooperated with the elite.[80] At other

---

77. Millett, *op. cit.* (1880), para. 189.
78. Benett, *op. cit.* (1870), para. 75.
79. Sleeman, *op. cit.*, I, 56.
80. Also see *ibid.*, II, 88.

times, properties were forcibly wrested from the raja's
former subordinate kinsmen despite their wish to retain
the autonomy they had gained under strong Muslim
rulers. In general, the talukas which the lineage elites
controlled at the time of British annexation bore little
relation to what they formerly had been. They consisted
mainly of those properties which the raja and elite had
managed to reacquire. Sometimes, however, powerful
lineage elites of the British period controlled talukas
much larger than those occupied by the lineage brethren
or those which had been in the past controlled by the
lineage elite. Lack of fit between kin boundary and proprietary boundary heightened the condition which characterized stages two and three. In stage two, the nonconformity is due to the conquest of foreign lineages by a
raja; in stage three it results from the redistricting of a
strong state which settled the revenue with village headmen; in stage four (*a*), it comes about through the recon-
stitution in an opportunistic fashion of the moribund
powers of the lineage elite.

Other personages besides the lineage raja and elite
profited from the anarchy of the times. Tax farmers,
courtiers, and government appointees all tried to pursue
their personal gain when the state faltered. Village headmen to whom the state had granted revenue engagement
rights as representatives of a corporate kin body of village
zamindars asserted proprietary superiority over their
brethren and attempted to reduce them to cultivator
status.[81] Often village zamindars pledged their proprietary
holdings to local strong men with whom they had no kin
relationship, but who could offer them protection through

81. Moreland, *op. cit.*, pp. 164–165. Moreland believed that such
occurences only transpired under British rule, and that headmen
never usurped proprietary positions in prior native states—an
idealized view of the traditional headman and his role vis à vis
the village community and the state.

court influence or other devices. Sometimes such new men coerced the village communities into obedience and proprietary subjugation. Tax farmers, courtiers, government appointees, and the traditional hereditary lineage elite were known to the British as talukdars, because they served as the link between state and local cultivators.[82]

Thus began an acrimonious, lengthy, and theoretically unresolved debate between the proponents of the talukdars as hereditary lineage heads and the supporters of the talukdars as mere tax farmers. The tenure situation which the British dealt with was incredibly confused, a true reflection of the anarchic political conditions which plagued the country before British annexation.

For example, in the Hardoi district, the early revenue authorities found that most talukdars were not of the old, "feudal" sort, but rather had come to their positions through purchase or by standing security for villages.[83] In the Lucknow district, Butts found that only two of twenty-three talukdars were old, hereditary landlords. Yet the situation was not quite so simple. Butts also noted that many of the remaining talukdars had some hereditary holdings, but had amassed the rest by transfer or revenue farming.[84] This mixture of part hereditary, part recently-acquired holdings confused the British. In their search for proof of true proprietorship, the British defined hereditary possession as legitimate but acquisition by force illegitimate.

Yet what in fact was the difference between the taluk-

---

82. Moreland wrote of this period: "Thus the first English administrators had to deal with Chiefs who were also Farmers, as well as with Farmers on the way to become Chiefs, and there is nothing surprising in the fact that for a time the two classes were treated as one." *Ibid.*, p. 173.

83. Baden-Powell, *op. cit.* (1892) II, 232.

84. H. H. Butts, *Report of the Land Revenue Settlement of the Lucknow District,* pp. 90–91.

dar whose possessions consisted of hereditary lineage lands
and the talukdar who purchased his powers or was a
revenue farmer? Benett believed little separated the two.
He felt that all talukdars were tax farmers differing only
in their social antecedents.[85] In one sense Benett was correct: hereditary lineage rajas who guaranteed the revenue
of their kinsmen and newly arisen tax farmers who stood
surety for the revenue as agricultural entrepreneurs were
both empowered and recognized by the central authority.
In this view, Benett stood in opposition to the school of
British revenue authorities who felt that the hereditary
talukdars were true feudal rulers and the tax farmers
were false johnnies-come-lately. Millett refers to these
categories as "pure" and "impure" talukdars, respectively.[86] This author believed that impure talukdars were
distinguishable by the absence of a large body of kinsmen
of the talukdar and the recency of the latter's tenure. But
tax farmer talukdars were "impure," only because insufficient time had elapsed for their lineages to proliferate
and for their possessions to be hallowed by hereditary
tradition.

Benett's position can be turned around so that it has
relevance from the perspective of the local level: all
talukdars were pure, all were the heads of bodies of kinsmen, all enjoyed possession on the basis of hereditary
principles. Some talukdars, however, were of recent origin
and therefore their lineages had not yet ramified into a
large number of cadet lines. The upheavals which led to
their ascendancy were still well remembered (especially
by recently dispossessed village zamindars). Other talukdars were of ancient derivation, their lineages had
branched out extensively, sometimes over a wide territory,
and the sharp dealings which had brought them to power

85. Benett, *op. cit.* (1870), para. 87.
86. Millett, *op. cit.* (1873), para. 139.

were forgotten. The recent talukdars owed their origins to state intervention in the local area during a time of strength, whereas the old talukdars had established themselves in a time of weakness. But once established, both old and new proceeded to increase their proprietary holdings in the same manner: they generated a new lineage body (although differing in scale) and over time, might become indistinguishable from each other. In terms of a developmental cycle, only one set of lineage principles exists which leads to the formation of local political groups; only one role of political preeminence and economic intermediation—whether it be called clan raja, talukdar, tax-farmer, or local adventurer.

(b) DECLINE TO YEOMAN-PEASANTRY

If state power remains strong in stage four, lineage organization becomes different from that outlined in the section above. Under a strong state, the removal of all preeminence in local lineages which was initiated by the state in stage three proceeds until the lineage elite and the village-level kinsmen are removed from their managerial and proprietary prerogatives. The literature refers to "republican" lineages. Such lineages had no rajas or elites, and were often represented to the central government in revenue dealings by relatively powerless delegates of the corporate kin body. The latter were individuals of no great wealth or status. Bhaiacharya tenure was often coupled with this republicanism or equality of mediocrity. Bhaiacharya tenure rarely extended to the division of revenue or produce but almost always referred to division of land.[87] However, because this tenure system required periodic redistribution of land in order to correct inequalities brought on by differential population increase

87. Cf. Baden-Powell, *op. cit.* (1892), I, 107.

over generations, lands were, in effect, held corporately by the participating kin group.

Such minutely divided republican lineages or "peasant proprietaries" seem to be the evolutionary end-product of a lineage under the strict control of a powerful state, where territorial expansion is impossible for political and ecological reasons. The absence of a frontier requires the lineage to proliferate steadily in a fixed area. Ancestral lands become progressively more divided, and the lineage populations are forced to take over increasing amounts of land under direct cultivation. The state removes the leaders or renders them powerless, as does the increasingly bleak economic situation within the lineage.

Oldham described the British settlement of the Ghazipur district as made on the basis of talukas. However, the settlement had no talukdars. Instead each estate contained a kin brotherhood consisting of many individual holders. Olham notes, "Settlements were concluded with a few headmen in each estate, as representative for the whole community." [88] These headmen were variously called *chaudharis, babus,* or *thakurs*—titles which do not reflect the preeminence of a lineage elite but at most the influence of a kin line which was first among equals and representative of the whole brotherhood.

One main weakness of such republican lineages and their chaudharis was their closeness to the land. The more reduced in position a lineage was, the more its members were forced to undertake their own cultivation (in a managerial sense; cultivation of sir usually did not require the actual labor of the village proprietor). The percentage of lands directly cultivated by the zamindar is high throughout the Banares region where the Rajput yeoman zamindar population is great. In Lakhnesar pargana of the Ballia district, home of a famous independent and unsub-

88. Oldham, *op. cit.,* part I, p. 41.

dued republican lineage—the Sengur Rajputs—50 per-
cent of the land was held as sir.[89] Further evolution led to
the lineage members becoming simple cultivators; their
former sir lands became the fields they held as occupancy
or privileged tenants. Land scarcity and lineage proliferation made the pattidari tenure system based on ancestral
shares (with its inherent inequalities of shares) difficult to
maintain.

The preceding pages have described two other points
in the lineage cycle when republican organization emerged
—both are instances of the regulation of a local lineage
by external powers against which it cannot defend itself.
In stage two, a lineage unable to expand its territory and
hemmed in by more powerful neighbors did not develop
a raja or elite. In the absence of a lineage hegemony and
through decreasing proprietary allotments per family,
such a lineage ended up as a highly fractionated republican kin body. An even more extreme evolution occurs in
stage two and four (*a*) when conquering rajas or talukdars
reduced their newly acquired subjects from managerial
positions to the condition of favored cultivators. Should a
powerful state set aside the elite intermediaries, the situation of stage four (*b*) would be achieved.

Although the cultivation of greater and greater amounts
of sir reflects a degenerating situation for individual zamindars, it also often leads to increased state land revenue.
This increased revenue was another reason why powerful
states tried to implement a policy which created such local
tenurial conditions.

At its extreme, stage four (*b*) sees two basic constituents
of political organization at the local level: the republican
Rajput lineages reduced to the role of somewhat privileged cultivators; and the local representatives of the

89. D. T. Roberts, *Report of the Revision of Records of Part
of Ballia District*, p. 32.

powerful state. In certain places, the state may give its revenue rights to farmers or court favorites. Unlike the situation of the upstart talukdars of stage four (*a*), these favorites had little, if any, connection with the local area. They rarely were able to carve out empires like the latter talukdars because of the strength of central authority. They were thus merely creatures of the state and beholden to it.

The British found such a lineage regime upon their initial occupation of the Banaras territory, the outcome of the state policy of the powerful rajas of Banaras. Such farmers and courtiers were generally set aside without qualms under company rule throughout the Banaras region and parts of the Conquered and Ceded Districts. This early conditioning may have misled the British in the situation which they met later in Oudh. The British first assumed that the Oudh talukdars were of the same caliber as the feeble revenue intermediaries they had found in the Banaras and Northwestern districts. The company officials failed to recognize that many of the Oudh talukdars were hereditary lineage heads; they also did not recognize the different structural relationship between state, talukdar, and village zamindar that typified stage four (*a*) in Oudh but which was not true of stage four (*b*) which they had encountered in the Banaras region and parts of the Northwestern Provinces.

I shall now detail the actions of the state in promoting the republican lineages of stage four (*b*). The rajas of Banaras, shortly before company takeover, pursued an aggressive state policy toward the village zamindars. The powerful Balwant Singh reduced the administrative and fiscal powers of the local kin brotherhoods and successfully removed all traces of economic and political precedence from internal lineage organization (see stage three).[90] In 1832, when the British investigated the subordinate rights of village zamindars, they found their powers surviving in only 600 out of 2000 estates.[91] Earlier, in 1790, Duncan speculated that of 5,000 zamindars in the Banaras province, 2,000 had been ejected by successive rajas.[92] As the rights of the village zamindars were crushed the position of the cultivator improved. The Banaras rajas tried to so reduce the village kin body that they became indistinguishable from their cultivator counterparts. British revenue authorities found *ryot* (cultivator) proprietary rights within the family domain of the raja of Banaras.[93] Muir comments that this situation results from the raja's leniency toward the cultivators as another avenue of attack on the village zamindars. Might not ryot proprietorship also have arisen from the reduction of the village zamindars to cultivator status without a total loss of their former proprietary privileges or at least retaining memory of them? [94]

What, in fact, happened when a powerful state authority dispossessed the village zamindars? Loss of zamin-

90. Oldham, *op. cit.*, part II, p. 93.

91. Muir, *op. cit.*, p. 75.

92. P. C. Wheeler, *Revision of Records and Settlement Operations in Jaunpur*, para. 185.

93. Muir, *op. cit.*, p. 71.

94. For example, Doaba pargana in the Ballia district was almost wholly owned by the maharaja of Dumraon. The original Rajput occupants of the Lautamia lineage had no proprietary rights, but were well off as tenants of the maharaja. Throughout the Banaras region, the position of tenants was high—in large measure, I suggest, because they were formerly village zamindars. Sleeman notes this causal sequence. He writes that dispossessed village proprietors in Oudh, "plundered of all they had in the world, and without any hope of redress, left the country, or took service under our Government, or that of Oude, or *descended to the rank of day-laborers or cultivators in other estates.*" (Emphasis mine.) Sleeman, *op. cit.*, II, 113.

dar status mostly meant loss of the prerogative of revenue collection to state officials. Apparently the system of revenue collection in the Banaras province shortly before Duncan's *lambardari* (or headman) settlement was of a *ryotwari* nature. Government officials—*amils*—collected directly and individually from each holder or *pattidar*. The Benares *Gazetteer* says that in 1808 the amils were banned from collecting directly from pattidars, perhaps because the expense proved too great.[95] The presence of such a ryotwari settlement was in keeping with the Banaras rajas' attempts to circumvent the village zamindars and go directly to the cultivators for revenue. Or, in the case of village zamindars who were also cultivators, it would effectively deny all superior status through the corporate kin group (which in military terms was the only threat the republican lineages could mount).

Even when village zamindars were replaced by state officials who took over the village revenue administration, they were allowed to keep their sir lands. They were also generally permitted certain special grazing, fishing, and forest rights, and they received a portion of the tax on liquor, houses, looms, and transport duties. They were often given various remissions and grants for support.[96] They were specifically denied, however, the right to collect revenue from the village tenants who were not members of the village kin body, and thus the zamindars lost control over lands not directly under their cultivation. Except for the special dispensations mentioned above and a preferential rate of land revenue, the village kin zamindars were not different from the other resident cultivators of the village.

Over time their condition might deteriorate further. If the kin body had no preferential control over subordinate

95. Wheeler, *op. cit.*, p. 81.
96. Oldham, *op. cit.*, part II, p. 94.

tenants, within a few generations holdings fragmented and lands were increasingly held as sir or directly cultivated. The increasing inequality of the ancestral shares and increasing external pressures requiring community solidarity sometimes resulted in the bhaiacharya tenures described above.

Baden-Powell, despite his knowledge of Indian land tenures, resisted the idea that bhaiacharya communities might be outgrowths of pattidari tenure. His perception of the Indian village and tenurial forms was heavily influenced by nineteenth century notions of social organization and racial or ethnic identities. For example, Baden-Powell believed that the severalty village form (non-corporate cultivators with separate holdings) was primary in India and connected it with Dravidian origins. Although he distinguished two different types of joint village, Baden-Powell ascribed both of them to the Aryan race. The two forms of joint village—pattidari and bhaiacharya—Baden-Powell thought indicative of different ethnic and historical situations. He believed that bhaiacharya tenures characteristically arose from the settlement of an Aryan clan or tribe throughout a territory, or as a result of the territorial dispersion of a clan over time. Baden-Powell argued that such ethnic or tribal settlements created a kin domain in which a clan raja did not preside, where "monarchial" qualities were absent, and where property was held under bhaiacharya tenure. Joint villages might also emerge through destruction of a kingdom and the rustification of the government elite, or through direct land grants from the sovereign to court favorites. A kin raja often existed and land was held in pattidari tenure. Because Baden-Powell associated these two types of joint villages with different ethnic and historical situations, he resisted the idea that pattidari tenures might give way to bhaiacharya tenures. He did not oppose a developmental viewpoint—for he believed, contrary to Maine, that the Dravidian severalty village gave way to the Aryan joint form. He simply felt that the clan origins behind bhaiacharya tenure precluded any development out of pattidari tenure.

Yet Baden-Powell provides evidence to contradict his antiquated notions of race and society and his outmoded evolutionism. He gives examples of Rajput rulerships, now destroyed and ruralized, which had adopted bhaiacharya tenure and which he admits as "virtually a clan settlement." Baden-Powell to some extent recognizes the arbitrary quality of his classification when he writes that "it is quite possible that village bodies really of individual foundation may have adopted the *bhaiacharya* method of equalized holdings usually observed in clan-settlements; and the latter may sometimes adopt the method of ancestral shares, which more commonly indicates descent from a single founder." Nevertheless, Baden-Powell persisted in the distinction between bhaiacharya and pattidari as representative of different ethnic and historical origins.

One of the reasons he felt that pattidari origins could be distinguished from bhaiacharya origins was the persistence of a sense of nobility and elevated descent among the impoverished cosharers. Baden-Powell notes: "in the course of a few generations, the descendant of the former Raja . . . is assimilated to the peasant grade . . . But though to alien eyes he is a mere peasant-proprietor, or village co-sharer, in his own eyes and also in those of his neighbors, his high caste and descent are still his own; and that makes all the difference." One of the differences, at least according to Baden-Powell, is the preservation of pattidari tenure based on ancestral shares.

In stage four (*b*) of the developmental cycle, preservation of corporate kin identity does lead to cooperation in resisting incursions on the lineage territory by outsiders (see below). Yet continued land fragmentation and pressure by a strong state may eventually outweigh persistent kin loyalties and introduce a bhaiacharya regime. Although Baden-Powell opposed this developmental sequence, he again provides examples of it. In parts of the Northwestern Provinces an unusual form of land tenure called *bighadam* existed. This tenurial system seems to reflect the adaptation of a pattidari system to increasing land inequalities, and represents a midpoint in the evolution from pattidari to bhaiacharya. If the land shares in an originally pattidari estate become unequal over time or if the shares vary greatly in value, it often becomes impossible for a cosharer to pay his portion of the land revenue from his allotted ancestral share. He answers his difficulties with the bighadam system in which each landholder pays a fraction of the land revenue proportional to his holdings rather than his ancestral share. Sometimes possession is figured in terms of acres, and sometimes as a fraction of the whole of the village lands. Baden-Powell suggests that eventually the latter fraction will come to represent the ancestral shares since the coparcenors never lose sight of their descent from a common ancestor. Baden-Powell ignores bighadam arrangements where the revenue is noted in acres rather than a fraction. In those areas the tenurial system is well on the way to bhaiacharya. Even where bighadam is expressed as a fraction of the whole, no justification exists for the belief that the system will be rationalized in the future on ancestral shares. Once the equalization of the revenue burden has been introduced into the tenurial system, it tends to abrogate all notions of ancestral shares since it introduces individual variation and readjustment in each generation. Finally, continued recognition of common descent has never stood in the way of the development of a bhaiacharya system. Common descent increasingly becomes a statement of ideology at the local level and decreasingly a determinant of tenurial arrangements.[97]

Baden-Powell's resistance to such notions was in keeping with his advocacy of the severalty village as historically primary in India. If bhaiacharya tenure can originate in pattidari forms, then the further evolution of bhaiacharya types into severalty (or ryotwari) forms is possible—a conclusion unacceptable to Baden-Powell. Yet bhaiacharya tenure is an intermediate stage between joint village (pattidari tenure) and severalty village (ryotwari tenure). Although both pattidari and bhaiacharya tenures assume proprietary brotherhood, the latter resembles ryotwari because of its separate holdings. Furthermore, bhaiacharya tenures are neither chartered nor encumbered by a system of ancestral shares—again a point of similarity with ryotwari forms. Might not bhaiacharya tenures represent the "missing link" in the evolution of severalty villages from joint ones (the sequence proposed by Maine)?

We need not take sides in the battle between Baden-Powell and Maine. The developmental cycle approach obviates this necessity. Bhaiacharya communities continue from stage four (*b*) into the regeneration of the lineage cycle (as will be made clear below), and represent both the oldest and youngest tenurial form. They are the degenerate endproduct of the Rajput lineage in stage four (*b*) and the original communities of cultivators to bear the conquest of the next round of lineage founders in stage one.

Without raja or elite and under extreme pressure from a powerful state in stage four (*b*), the position of the republican lineages is greatly depressed. Only one protective device stands between them and total absorption into the cultivator class—their corporate pugnacity. Reduced to

97. See Baden-Powell, *The Indian Village Community*, pp. 225–327, and *Village Communities in India*, p. 70.

the lowest level of economic and political cohesion, sentiments of kinship could still be summoned in the form of armed bodies of village lineage mates.[98] Although these were no match for an organized, well-disciplined, and well-equipped army, such village-level pugnacity operated like a mosquito militia: too small to make a full army campaign worthwhile; too large, however, to be undone by a small party of revenue officials. When republican lineages lost this pugnacity (which was to a large extent based on the large lineage populations that exacerbated their weakness), they were overwhelmed and sold out to farmers and revenue bidders selected by the state, or managed directly by central revenue officials.

The same process by which the state introduced foreigners into the administrative machinery of local areas in stage three characterized stage four (*b*) except the process was intensified. The powerful state had been so successful in removing lineage preeminence that the only resistance to its intrusions was the local defensive pugnacity of the village kinsmen. Courtiers, revenue farmers, and state officials began the process of building up their local influence, at the same time as their personal lineage proliferated, ramified, and divided (either territorially or in terms of revenue receipts) the lands which formed the original state grant or purchase. With time and success, such foreigners grew to resemble the lineage organization of the former Rajput proprietary bodies. As such lineages increased, they put mounting pressure on their original holdings. Consequently they attempted to reduce former village zamindars to cultivators. This evolution is similar to that described in four (*a*), except that the increased strength of the state permits new superordinate lineages of state appointees smaller chance of success.

98. See Cohn, *op. cit.*, pp. 92, 94, 98 for various examples.

STAGE FIVE

ANARCHY AND REGENERATION OF THE CYCLE

The full round of the lineage developmental cycle depends on the weakening of the central power after a time of strength. Anarchy threatens the local area when the state becomes weak. State weakness sets off power struggles between local strong men who are no longer hampered by the restraints of a powerful state. Havoc and destruction of cultivation result, as people throw up their agricultural pursuits and run for safety or adopt more mobile pursuits such as banditry. The weakening of the state opens up an internal territorial frontier by creating wastelands, promoting famine, pillage and armed confrontations leading to depopulation, and spreading epidemics which also reduce the population. During stage four (*a*) or at the end of stage four (*b*), the adventurer-freebooter returns, ready to lay claim to lands recently left uncultivated, ready to attract tenants under guarantee of protection and ready to carve out a territory in which his lineage can spread and proliferate. These adventurers may be the old hereditary elites of stage four (*a*) who have survived still another political upheaval; they may be the government appointees who have proved successful in the political interregnum; they may be the advance guard of the next state authority which will try to subdue the territory; or they may be the bandit-adventurers of stage three come to conquer new lands. The result is a return to the conditions of stage one, in which the presence of a territorial frontier and the absence of state control combine to promote the fortunes of enterprising men. Such individuals establish their kin bodies in a local area from which they will spread outward through genealogical fissioning. Eventually, they populate a region in which they form a series of lineage confederacies or village proprietaries.

The lineage developments of stage four (*a*) and their continuation under increasingly anarchic conditions in stage five complete the circle in the Rajput developmental cycle. The hereditary talukdars seeking to reclaim their patrimony and the upstart talukdars carving out their proprietary rights by force and purchase represent the *in situ* evolution of lineage founders described in stage one. As state control weakens, adventures come to the fore in their local area. Most of the new talukdars have little connection with the locality. Those who are rejuvenated lineage rajas so plunder and extort to achieve political success that they soon stand at great remove from their disenfranchised village kinsmen. Whether through devolution of their state offices and state land grants or evolution from lineage headship, such men operate within the context of their minimal lineages. Later, their proliferating lineage will begin to spread over wide territories and to form the supra-lineage confederacies described in stage one.

A somewhat different course leads to the regeneration of the developmental cycle from stage four (*b*). Lineage founders immigrate into an area from outside and subordinate the former lineage proprietors (now reduced to cultivators) to their own political domination. These migrants, who are perhaps the dispossessed lineage elites of stage three forced from their ancestral homes, correspond to the lineage situation of stage one as introduced by nonlocal adventurers. The corporate, kin-linked village zamindars of stages two and three thus evolve into the highly fragmented, kin-ramified, sir-cultivating peasant proprietors of stage four (*b*). The latter, in turn, are the seed of the noncorporate, nonproprietary village agriculturalists of a new stage one. Exploited by a lineage raja in stage two, favored by the state in stage three, and finally dispossessed by central authority in stage four (*b*), the former village zamindars become the local cultivators conquered and taxed by the lineage founders of stage one.

In any situation, a mixture between resident and immigrant lineage founders existed. Their geographical origins are less important than the common relationship in which they stood to the depressed former lineages below and the weak or debilitated state above. This common status rejuvenates the lineage developmental cycle, and sets in train the successive stages of lineage dominance and decline, and of state intrusion and repulse in the local area.

A developmental cycle has no end, except one brought on by such a massive social rearrangement that the traditional circularity is irrevocably broken. Baden-Powell and Maine argued about the original type of village organization of Hindu rural life. Maine believed the beginning point was the corporate proprietary brotherhood of village zamindars, the so called "joint village." Rural settlements which did not have such a cooperative, joint body of village zamindars had been rent asunder by anarchy, British revenue systems, or other abnormal conditions.[99] Baden-Powell held the opposite view. He saw the so-called "severalty" villages consisting of noncorporate cultivators, each tied to his own plot (which was not determined by ancestral shares) as primary and prior to the joint village type. The latter arose through alienation of state revenue to courtiers and court favorites, which introduced them into the rural area as a class of superior tenure-holders. Or, joint villages might come about through tribal conquests, when the original cultivators were totally subordi-

99. Henry Sumner Maine, *Village Communities in East and West*, p. 123.

nated and reduced to tenants by the invaders. Baden-Powell conceived these as evolutions from the earliest Indian village and state form: that is, a group of noncorporate cultivators, each directly working his own demarcated fields and paying land revenue to a nonrelated chief or raja without the intercession of any intermediary.[100]

We may chastise Maine and Baden-Powell for the folly of believing in a single original type of village and proprietary form. Their misconceptions arose partly from an unfortunate confusion of social form with racial stock. They spoke of stereotyped village forms in conjunction with Aryan and Dravidian races. Ultimately, they both seem to have been right—but also wrong: right in the sense that the two basic village forms they argued for appear both primary and then derivative, the one from the other, through the course of a developmental cycle. Maine and Baden-Powell were both wrong, however, in that their intellectual contest ossified around the purely structural question of which came first. Rather, they should have pursued the processural inquiry of how one village form unendingly developed into the other, like Vishnu's tail-in-mouth snake, Sesha.

This chapter has attempted to set the Rajput stratified lineage into a diachronic framework through the use of a developmental cycle model. The employment of a cyclical model helps avoid many definitional problems of what a lineage really was, by recognizing that at different stages it was different things. Because the British revenue authorities tried to stereotype the Rajput lineage they often invented spurious distinctions such as those between pure and impure talukdars. The developmental cycle explored in this chapter also helps identify the important and perhaps causal factors underlying the different organizational

100. Baden-Powell, *op. cit.* (1896), pp. 103ff., 110–111, 183, 205.

stages of the Rajput stratified lineage. Most generally, it defines the interactional context in which local level political groups were linked to the state and demonstrates how local kin bodies responded to alterations in the power of central authorities and their intrusions into the local political scene.

4

KINSHIP AND THE STATE

Kinship withers as society passes from the primitive to the complex. Familial etiquette gives way to class and power relationships. Lineage and clan are by-passed in favor of county, province, and state.

Since Lewis Henry Morgan,[1] this thesis has been the dictum of many anthropologists. In their study of African political systems, Fortes and Evans-Pritchard distinguish centralized polities ("Group A") from acephalous kin societies ("Group B"). They write:

One of the oustanding differences between the two groups is the part played by the lineage system in political structure. [In societies of Group A, the] political unit is essentially a territorial grouping wherein the plexus of kinship ties serves merely to cement those already established by membership

1. Morgan spoke of a passage from societies based on kinship to those based on territory. See Lewis Henry Morgan, *Ancient Society*, p. 6.

of the ward, district, and nation. . . . In societies of Group B the segmentary lineage system primarily regulates political relations between territorial segments.[2]

More recently, Fried stated:

A state is not simply a legislature, an executive body, a judiciary system, an administrative bureaucracy, or even a government . . . a state is better viewed as the complex of institutions by means of which the power of the society *is organized on a basis superior to kinship.* . . . To the extent that a stratified [state] society lacks formal and specialized mechanisms of control it courts disaster, for in the face of weakening bonds of kinship, in face of the commonplace realization that the web of kin cannot contain the enlarged population or the increasing number of others, of non-kinsmen in the society, it becomes a question of developing formal, specialized instruments of coercion.[3]

The belief that kinship and state are institutions of wholly different provenance is also evident in the following statement from the sociologist Lenski:

Among societies at an advanced horticultural level of development, the separation of the political and kinship systems and the resulting development of the state *are necessary preconditions for the development of marked social inequality.*[4]

In a recent paper on African kingdoms, Peter Lloyd criticized the political classification of African societies employed by Fortes and Evans-Pritchard, and implied

2. M. Fortes and E. E. Evans-Pritchard, *African Political Systems,* p. 6.
3. Morton H. Fried, *The Evolution of Political Society,* pp. 229–230. (Emphasis mine.)
4. Gerhard Lenski, *Power and Privilege: A Theory of Social Stratification,* p. 160. (Emphasis in original.)

skepticism concerning the incompatibility of kinship and state. Lloyd writes:

> In criticism of Evans-Pritchard and Fortes, it was soon pointed out that in not all the "stateless" societies is the segmentary lineage the basis of political organization . . . nor is the lineage an unimportant social group in the "states." Yet the division into states and stateless societies has been upheld by successive writers and the concepts of segmentation, lineage, centralization, and the state have dominated attempts at classification. As set out, these concepts form dichotomized pairs—segmentation v. centralization, lineage v. the state.[5]

The incongruity between the principles of kin-based societies and those of state societies is a valid theoretical distinction which highlights the direction of social change. In their extreme forms, the organization of a complex state bears little relationship to the institutions promoting cohesion in acephalous kin societies.

Another question remains, however: What is the role of kinship and kin institutions in the *development* of state society and centralized political domains? Morgan and the scholars quoted above understand that no sharp revolutionary leap changes the familial system into the state-territorial systems. Rather, kinship is slowly extinguished; it grows jejune as the state increasingly intrudes on its political, economic, and social functions. and private property and the rule of coercive force replace communal holdings and the custom of kin allegiance. As the evolution of

5. Peter C. Lloyd, "The Political Structure of African Kingdoms: An Exploratory Model" in *Political Systems and the Distribution of Power* (Association of Social Anthropologists monograph no. 2), p. 65. Lloyd goes on to cite anthropologists such as Fortes, Fallers, and Mair who use this distinction between kin and state. The concept of kinship employed by Fortes, Evans-Pritchard, and other anthropologists concerns corporate unilineal descent groups. Throughout this study, I have also used the word kinship to refer to such genealogically-based *corporate* groups.

state society proceeds, kinship becomes a shabby remnant of its former self, a relic of tribal times, and an impediment to the unified state because it promotes regional sentiments that engender dissent.

The view that sees kinship as the sluggish, soon-to-be-extinct dinosaur of state societies does not seem to fit the Rajputs of northern India; nor does it seem to fit the process of state formation in other societies. In this study I wish to advance a processural viewpoint unlike the structural generalizations of Morgan and the other authorities quoted above: Why should not the *process* of state evolution out of a kin-tribal heritage incorporate along the way many social institutions which in the final structural transformation disappear or sharply atrophy? Although kinship and state may be in opposition structurally, may not genealogical institutions gradually pave the way for the formation of centralized political domains?

This question forms the primary focus of the following pages. The chapter evaluates the role of kinship in the formation of the state, and examines how kin and clan undertake many political activities within state polities. This investigation will, I hope, validate the foregoing Rajput materials as an exercise in comparative political anthropology. Use of kin groups in local administration is not unique to the North Indian state. Through analysis of other state societies, the role of kin organization in the development of state forms may be more adequately expressed, and some general conclusions concerning the formation of the state may be advanced.

The enduring controversy over the role of kinship in North Indian state society indicates the manner in which kin-state organization can be misunderstood by outmoded cultural evolutionary notions and European historical chauvinism. Material drawn from various "tribal" peoples of the Indian subcontinent will illustrate the nature of a viable "kin-feudated" state. The analogous case of medieval Irish society, as presented by Maine, will give comparative depth to the presentation, and also indicate at least one of the ways in which kin-based polity is successfully abrogated. The Irish data also lead to an investigation of the role of kin groups in the organization of centralized, territorial states. Archaeological findings from Aztec, Inca, and Mesopotamian states confirm the preservation (at least initially) of the kin order within a centralized domain. The Indian and Irish tribal materials indicate polities analogous to the internal organization of the Rajput stratified lineage. The Aztec, Inca, and Mesopotamian data reflect the more complex situation of the Rajput lineage after its incorporation into a territorial state.

KINSHIP AND FEUDALISM IN INDIA

Tod, in his masterful study of Rajput polity in Rajasthan (Rajputana), introduced the notion that Indian social forms were similar to the feudal organization of Europe. He drew a comparison between the rajadoms of Western India and the dukedoms and feudal system of medieval Europe.[6] Other scholars have forthrightly denied the Rajput polities of Rajasthan the status of feudal states because of the web of kinship which bound the state raja to his political subordinates. They thus indirectly argue against the importance of kinship in the North Indian state, and view its presence as a devolutionary or tribal phenomenon. For instance, Lyall wrote:

Even Colonel Tod, whose intimate knowledge of Rajputana has been never equalled . . . has been so far misled by the likeness as to miss the radical distinction between the two

6. James Tod, *Annals and Antiquities of Rajasthan.*

forms of society, tribal and feudal . . . Perhaps we should not blame him for failing to see that his Rajput feudalism was not the basis of the society, but an incomplete superstructure, and that Rajputana . . . was a group of tribal suzerainities rapidly passing into the feudal stage, which we now know to have been largely built up in Europe over the tribal foundations . . . the cement of the system was something much stronger than feudalism.[7]

Suzanne Rudolph has rightly criticized Lyall's implicit stereotyping of evolutionary stages in political organization.[8] How else could the distinction between tribal and feudal polity be accepted so readily? An antiquated evolutionism, however, does not underlie Thorner's recent acceptance of Lyall's position.[9] Thorner accepts the distinction between tribal political structure (based on kin groups) and feudal political organization as valid. But suppose, however, this distinction is not significant to the society at hand? Is it merely unconscious ethnocentrism which creates the assumption that kinship polity and feudal polity are necessarily mutually exclusive? Thorner presents an excellent case, as did Lyall and Tod before, for viewing European feudalism and the Rajput principalities as closely related political patterns. But suppose that the organizational quality of a foreign polity which makes it appear alien to a European analyst is also the quality that the analyst writes off as being more primitive or tribal in comparison with the polities he knows? One would have to conclude that the analyst has failed to recognize the comparative significance of foreign organi-

7. Alfred Lyall, *Asiatic Studies, Religious and Social,* p. 212.
8. Suzanne Rudolph, "The Princely States of Rajputana: Ethic, Authority, and Structure," *Indian Journal of Political Science,* XXIV (1963), 20.
9. Daniel Thorner, "Feudalism in India," in R. Coulborn ed., *Feudalism in History,* pp. 133–155 *passim.*

zational forms. The same, it appears, has happened with kinship and polity in India. If genealogical reckoning could be ignored as a tribal pattern, its occurrence beside sophisticated state political institutions did not jeopardize general theories of feudalism or state organization. The importance of kinship as an organizational principle in India beyond the family and village was also not apprehended.

Rushton Coulborn exemplifies this attitude. He believes that feudalism analogous to European feudalism existed in preindustrial India.[10] For Coulborn, Thorner's kinship connections between state ruler and local chiefs only emerge during the decline of the original feudal structure. Coulborn points to the Japanese feudal system in which various family terms masked the essentially feudal relationships between individuals. Thus a feudal "family" in traditional Japan consisted of a lord and his retainers who had no real genealogical connection. In India, Coulborn says, the Rajputs described by Tod perceived that they were of the same clan as their raja. But they had only come to believe this as a result of decadence and "excessive emphasis upon caste (varna) [sic]."[11] Coulborn is not entirely wrong if his position can be understood in terms of vague categories of similar status based on kinship (such as "Chauhan"). Clearly kinship was often used to cover political relationships having little genealogical significance. But Coulborn has more in mind: implicit are general notions about the nature of political society and feudalism—notions which do not include kinship in any capacity other than symptomatic of decline and decadence. Yet even a political category such as Chauhan has

10. Rushton Coulborn, "Feudalism, Brahmanism, and the Intrusion of Islam upon Indian History," *Comparative Studies in Society and History*, X (1968), 370.

11. *Ibid.*, p. 371.

a kinship reference; even the overtly political is phrased in kinship terms.

How does Coulborn demonstrate concurrence of decadence and kinship phraseology in the political fortunes of northern India? He cites evidence of a time when the truly feudal Indian baronage—the ancestors of the latter-day Rajputs—had formed strong fiefs which were later reduced to kin territories and groups recognizing common kinship. Coulborn proves his hypothesis with extracts from Elliot's discussion of a grouping of eighty-four villages, commonly found throughout northern India, and generally referred to as a *chaurasia* (chaurasi = eighty-four).[12] A dubious attitude can be taken toward this proof of kinship as decadent feudalism. For the chaurasia is nothing more than another word for the pargana or taluka consisting of a stratified patrilineage claiming Rajput or other dominant caste status.[13] Rather than an elemental feudal domain, the chaurasia is a conventional number of villages all belonging to the same stratified lineage; it is the locus of North Indian kin and political confluence. The fact that Coulborn uses as proof of his "feudalism without kinship" thesis the local social unit which demonstrates genealogical reckoning, indicates that the two institutions are not separable in northern India. To be sure, Coulborn's limited definition of feudalism views it as a system of patron-client contractual relations. He might argue that the chaurasia was not a fief if it was a kin-defined territory. Leach has referred to this kind of typological thinking as "butterfly collecting." Coulborn avoids precisely what must be explained. For kin forms in North

12. *Ibid.*, p. 372.
13. H. M. Elliott, *Memoirs on the History, Folk-lore and Distribution of the Races of the N.W.P., Being an Amplified Edition of the Original Supplemental Glossary of Indian Terms by the Late Sir H. M. Elliot*, pp. 47ff.

India were employed to define, simulate, and mask ties of political clientage.

Coulborn has inverted the order of development. Rather than decadence contributing to the formation of kin jurisdictions and kin affect, the evolution of the state and its organization at the local level is intimately tied into the kinship order and its demarcated territory. What Coulborn sees as a period of "real" feudal baronage is perhaps the early stage of a stratified lineage which has not proliferated but stands as a small isolated familial body above a large number of cultivators whom it taxes. Such conditions exist in the initial stages of state formation rather than during its decline.

The Rajput materials from Rajasthan have become obscured and incumbered rather than illuminated by the decades of scholarly debate. Too much attention has been focused on the question of feudalism. Too little concern has been shown for the underlying principles of political organization at work in these polities. Other studies, however, have dealt with the organizational role of kinship in South Asian state formation. Curiously, such discussions have been limited to tribal societies which stood apart from the great bureaucratic empires of northern India. Wills in the early years of this century investigated traditional political organization on the Chattisgarh plateau in central India.[14] More recently, Sinha analysed the process of state formation among tribal peoples of Barabhum (also in central India).[15] These works clearly indicate the relevance of kinship for political behavior and state structure. Yet because the local situation lacked the

14. C. U. Wills, "The Territorial System of the Rajput Kingdoms of Medieval Chattisgarh," *Journal and Proceedings of the Asiatic Society of Bengal*, New Series XV (1919), 197–262.

15. Surajit Sinha, *State Formation and Rajput Myth in Tribal Central India.*

complexity of tenures, powers, and economic divisions of the Ganges plain, and because local society did not have the feudal ethic of noblesse oblige and status trappings, these works have not been sufficiently appreciated.

These studies show that local political groups based on kinship existed outside the Gangetic plain and Rajasthan. They show that lineage and genealogical organization is a significant aspect of political structure in traditional northern India, rather than just a unique artifact of Rajput tribalism. In a more general and comparative sense, the studies discussed below illustrate a type of state society still heavily dependent on genealogical struts. Examination of their institutional arrangements and response to social change helps redefine Thorner and Lyall's distinction between tribalism and feudalism and helps create a more meaningful comparison of different types of state orders. Wills's and Sinha's Indian studies, and Maine's work on ancient Irish society, will demonstrate how independent kin-based states evolve into complex, centralized polities. The latter eventually destroy the kin bodies which give them origin, and thus ultimately substantiate the structural discontinuity between kin institutions and state institutions.

KIN-FEUDATED STATES

At the time of initial British contact in 1770, the Bhumij state of Barabhum contained nine *tarafs* or political divisions. The raja of Barabhum ruled over this domain. The raja claimed Kshatriya Rajput status, controlled the state government, and directly administered the largest taraf. A second taraf, the smallest in number of villages, was set aside for the raja's eldest son. The remaining seven tarafs were governed by taraf *sardars*. The latter had strong powers within their individual jurisdictions, and came to the raja's aid in times of foreign military threat or when extraordinary funds were required. The raja, however, had no privileges of taxation and seemingly enjoyed limited coercive powers over the taraf sardars. The raja's main income, as that of his taraf subordinates, came from direct administration of his particular taraf.[16]

A territorial subdivision of the taraf existed in two of the larger tarafs. This unit, known as a *sadiyal*, had its own leader. The smallest administrative entity was the village. Villages were represented by headmen called *ghatwal*. Within villages certain individuals held leases over the most fertile lands in return for providing military service to the ghatwal, sadiyal or taraf sardar.[17]

Two earlier commentators on the Bhumij state, Dalton and Risley, both believed that its unusual political structure arose from a tribal background. They theorized that originally four tarafs existed, each ruled by a different Bhumij clan, but all sharing a common ancestry. The raja was merely the descendant of the oldest agnatic line of the original clan.[18] Sinha's data do not substantiate the Risley-Dalton interpretation, but he is not willing to reject it completely. Sinha reports, however, that today the Bhumij do not regard the tarafs as anything other than governmental administrative divisions with no kinship basis. Some fifty Bhumij clans are found in the Barabhum region, none of which are territorially isolated at any level. Taraf sardars, however, come from the most influential Bhumij clan in their taraf.[19]

Dalton's and Risley's hypothesis on the origin of the Bhumij political structure, and Sinha's notes on present-day organization, represent in large measure lineage or-

16. *Ibid.*, p. 44.
17. *Ibid.*
18. *Ibid.*, p. 45.
19. *Ibid.*, p. 46.

ganization in stage one of the developmental cycle presented above. The various tarafs are the original territorial acquisitions governed by several confederated kin heads, each having descended genealogically from a single lineage ancestor. The taraf sardars illustrate the successful cadet lines which are able to carve out independent empires during periods of weak state control or when frontiers existed. In stage one of the developmental cycle, little or no kin connection exists between the conquering lineage and the cultivators who are below it. The relationship between the taraf sardars and the Bhumij village clans appears similar, although Sinha is not clear in this matter. Perhaps sufficient time had not elapsed in Barabhum for larger ruling kin bodies to arise, except those exemplified by the *sadiyals*. It is no wonder that the Bhumij saw the taraf as a legal-administrative division with political significance rather than a lineage-based segment. The lineage principle was only operative within the limited sphere of the ruling elite.

Lack of an external state administration beyond the local raja distinguishes Bhumij state organization sharply from the Rajput lineage cycle. C. U. Wills's material on the aboriginal political organization of Chattisgarh pictures a state originally very similar to the Bhumij, and describes the consequences for indigenous political organization of foreign conquest by a preindustrial centralized regime. The sequence of events in Chattisgarh also duplicates the developmental cycle of Rajput lineages.

Wills describes the political structure of Chattisgarh as a state apparatus superimposed on a tribal base.[20] Three temporal and developmental stages characterize Chattisgarh. The first is the aboriginal organization before Rajput conquest and Mahratta domination. Wills' recon-

20. Wills, *op. cit.*, p. 255.

struction visualizes many separate tribal or clan territories, each headed by a republican leader who stood in agnatic relationship to his clan mates or tribal brethren. Each of these tribal or clan divisions is further segmented into kin-based subtribes or subclans, all of these again led by a kin-determined leader. Finally, each village was separately governed by a village headman, who descended in direct agnatic line from the original village leader. A series of such tribal or clan units was bound together politically under a superordinate leader. However, the leader did not have much power either at the tribe level or at the supratribe level. Nor did he enjoy a separate residence, retainers, or property other than the ancestral fields which he directly cultivated.[21] This political structure resembles the Rajput lineages of stage five, except for the absence of a superior bureaucratic authority. Note, however, the absolute conformity between kin territory and political influence in the hypothesized aboriginal Chattisgarh polity. This continuity, which is also seen in the early and late stages of the Rajput cycle was increasingly abrogated by the successive conquerors of this region. Whether a cyclical development occurred in aboriginal Chattisgarh, however, is impossible to judge on the basis of the scanty materials available.

The next stage of political development in Chattisgarh occurred about A. D. 1000 with the presumed conquest by Rajputs. Wills ascribes gradual changes in local polity to this event, but does not provide proof of this presumably pugnacious migration.[22] This stage might equally well have been a purely local development from the "tribal" organization above, just as among the Bhumij, rajas arose from *in situ* developments. The Rajput rulers of Chattisgarh might have emulated the Rajput model much

21. *Ibid.*, pp. 227–230.
22. *Ibid.*, pp. 233–244.

as their counterpart, the Bhumij raja of *Barabhum* did at a later date. Here again, the data are not sufficient to reach definite conclusions. If, however, the evolution of the Chattisgarh state proceeded from local events rather than a Rajput migration, then the organization of the polity described below can help us understand the political genealogy of the Bhumij state, which it so closely resembles.

Chattisgarh under the Rajputs consisted of a northern and a southern kingdom, with separate, independent rajas. Each kingdom was subdivided into *garhs* or districts, all of which pledged allegiance to the Rajput kingdom as a whole. Each of the two Chattisgarh rajas was conventionally assigned eighteen garhs. A *diwan* or *thakur* ruled a garh and owed only minimal duties to the raja. The garh was conventionally said to contain eighty-four villages, whence came their alternate name of chaurasia. Each garh was subdivided into talukas, conventionally composed of twelve villages. These villages were ruled by *daos* or *barhainihas* who exercised the same powers as the garh thakur or diwan, but on the local level. Below the level of the taluka stood the individual village communities, each represented and led by a headman.[23]

At times the garh chieftains were kinsmen of the raja. Sometimes the rulers of talukas were related to the leaders of the garhs. Village headmen often traced descent to the heads of their talukas. The system resembles Rajput polity in Rajasthan as described by Lyall to the extent that kinship linked the garh chieftain to the taluka leader and the village headman.[24] The web of kinship linking the various grades of society was the principle of polity in medieval Chattisgarh. Kinship was often abrogated, however, by actions of the raja. For example, the ruler introduced settlers from upper India and gave them lands

23. *Ibid.*, p. 199.
24. Cf. Lyall, *op. cit.*, pp. 207–211.

which had been taken from their original, pre-Rajput inhabitants—a situation similar to stage two of the Rajput developmental cycle in which the lineage elite introduces bodyguards and other followers from outside the kin sphere as independent sources of power and military threat.[25]

Wills, in a fashion similar to Lyall's, portrays the latter days of Rajput rule in Chattisgarh as an evolution from the tribal to the feudal. The pre-Rajput indigenous organization was almost completely kin-based. However, decreasing kinship between social grades, and the introduction of new social elements by the raja, gave the Rajput polity an increasingly "feudal" cast. Nevertheless, Wills concludes that the system was still predominantly familial. Although kinship between ruler and ruled had weakened, the political system still depended on genealogical status, not "feudal" contract.[26]

The third stage of political development in Chattisgarh witnesses the arrival of a conquering territorial state. In 1741, elements of the Mahratta empire overran the plateau with little resistance. The first goal of the centralized Mahratta administration was the elimination of all revenue and political intermediaries between the state and the actual cultivator. The Mahrattas shortly began to set aside the rajas, thakurs, and daos in a style similar to that of a powerful state in stage three of the Rajput developmental cycle.[27] This development had to some extent been presaged by the Chattisgarh Rajput rulers'

25. Wills, *op. cit.*, p. 244.
26. *Ibid.*, pp. 248, 250.
27. *Ibid.*, pp. 250–251. The indigenous elite were thrown out in favor of Brahmans who were officially called *patels*. Their duties and powers were similar to the old talukdars, but did not have the latter's longstanding attachment to the land or kin connections. The patels of Chattisgarh resemble the courtiers and state appointees of stage three and four (*b*) in the Rajput developmental cycle.

creation of a personal following outside the kin context. The Mahratta state represented only a more rapid and evolved instance of what Wills referred to as the "feudal-ization" of Chattisgarh.

We must turn to ancient and medieval Irish polities described by Maine to fully gauge the social evolution which Wills termed feudal. Irish polity represents a state form in all respects similar to those of Barabhum and Chattisgarh. It also resembles the Rajput lineages of stage one and two (apart from their domination by a centralized territorial state). Furthermore, the evolution from "tri-bal" forms to "feudalism" in India as conceived by Lyall and Wills also occurred in Ireland. Irish data helps ex-plain in more detail what happened to the kin-based order of Chattisgarh and similar occurrences during stage two of the Rajput lineage cycle.

Tribes in ancient and medieval Ireland were bodies of kinsmen claiming descent from a real or mythical ancestor. At the widest levels of tribal integration, genea-logical connection was often lacking. But at the level of the *sept* or subtribe, common ancestry was a historical fact.[28] A tribe was led by a chief, who was generally chosen from among the eligible males (usually adult) of the senior-most agnatic line of the tribe. The tribal fabric and the institutions of political leadership were thus both heavily grounded in a genealogical framework.

The territory inhabited by an Irish tribe was said to belong to the entire kin body. However, in reality great tracts were held in severalty by different lineages of tribal brethren.[29] A separate section of tribal lands accrued to the chief as his *demesne*—that is, he controlled it as an appurtenance of his office. This land was inherited from

28. Henry Sumner Maine, *Lectures on the Early History of Institutions,* pp. 90–91.
29. *Ibid.,* p. 92.

chief to chief without partition, and therefore passed down over the generations in a manner different from the proprietary succession which characterized the rest of the tribe.[30]

The description of the Irish tribe does not differ markedly thus far from the tribal polities of Barabhum and Chattisgarh, or the Rajput lineages of northern India in stages one and two of the developmental cycle. However, Maine describes various structural changes in Irish society which magnified the powers of the tribal chief over his fellow kinsmen, and which created classes of disenfranchised and disinherited men who were exploited by the tribal chief.

Evidence exists that some tribes were conquered and wholly subordinated to others.[31] External conquest, however, was not the major factor behind the growth of an exploitative, autocratic tribal chief. Rather, Maine points to several factors producing internal political and economic stratification in Ireland: First, the process of "commendation" by which free kinsmen become the chief's "vassals": Second, the chief's authority over waste lands and the servile colonies he planted there: Third, the growing strength of his retainers who come from outside the kin body.

Plow cattle rather than land was the major scarce resource in ancient and medieval Ireland. Tribal chiefs often controlled large herds of cattle which they willingly placed with their inferior kinsmen for use in tillage.[32] Several forms of contract, varying in severity and exploitation, existed to regulate the loan of cattle between chief and kinsman-commoner. Maine believes that vassalage in the Irish tribe originated when tribal free-

30. *Ibid.*
31. *Ibid.*, p. 133.
32. *Ibid.*, p. 158.

men were forced to accept this chiefly "gift," and therefore placed themselves in commendation to the tribal
ruler.

According to early Irish law a vassalage contract should
occur only between a tribesman and his kin chief. Often,
however, individuals contracted with foreign chiefs.[33]
Over time, subordinates and dependents grew up around
the tribal chief outside the kinship context. Access to such
followers gave the chief a new source of power which
freed him from dependence on his own tribal brethren.
The same development occurred in stage two of the
Rajput developmental cycle with the conquest of foreign
lineages.

Still another factor led to increasing social stratification within the Irish tribes. By custom, the tribal chief
had managerial and allocative rights over the waste lands
within the tribal territory. Such land control was of little
significance until a class of people emerged who could be
put to work on them. These were the "broken men"—
those who through misdeed had been outcaste from their
original tribal group and were forced to fend for themselves. Broken men formed an important element of the
Irish population.[34] They generally bound themselves to a
foreign chief who settled them as dependents on the waste
lands of his tribe. In this way the tribal chief replaced
the tribe or family as the guarantor of the safety and survival of such broken men.[35] Because these individuals had
no one except the chief to turn to, the tribal ruler was
free to rackrent and exploit them.

In the sixteenth century, English observers noted the
great cruelty, extortion, and exploitation practiced by
Irish chiefs. Maine believes that such behavior was not

33. *Ibid.*, pp. 164–165.
34. *Ibid.*, p. 174.
35. *Ibid.*, p. 183.

directed at their tribal brethren but at the rapidly increasing class of broken men. This increase came about through several centuries of anarchy and civil strife brought on by Danish piracy, internal feuds, and English attempts at conquest.[36] As tribes were disrupted, more broken men appeared. As chiefs provided protection to increasing numbers of nonkinsmen, the social differentiation within Irish society grew.

The Bhumij of Barabhum, the states of Chattisgarh, and the ancient Irish tribes have many things in common with the Rajput stratified lineages of northern India. Kinship and genealogical reckoning are the fundamental cement of all these political structures. From kinship comes the disposition of territory, the selection of chiefs, the order of status precedence, and the organization of military contingents. Various processural developments or institutions associated with the Rajput cycle have also appeared in Barabhum, Chattisgarh, and Ireland. Each of these kin-feudated polities is characterized by a great dispersion of political power. The chief is first among equals. His jurisdiction is strongest within his own lands or demesne. Subordinate princes rule independently as chiefly surrogates within their own kin-determined domains. Overall, the most significant characteristic of the kin-feudated type is that little political power is available outside the kinship system in the aboriginal or traditional framework. A chief holds office as the chosen one from the senior agnatic line of the tribe. Should the kin leader prove too demanding of his kinsmen, they can refuse to give him military service, withhold their customary gifts, sunder the ties of kin etiquette which bind their allegiance to him, leave to join another tribe or lineage, or depose him in favor of a pretender-relative.

The aboriginal situation may change, however. Among

36. *Ibid.*

the Chattisgarhi tribes, Wills reported a gradual lessening of the ties of kinship. Maine noted the growth of the Irish chief independent of his kinsmen, with his own source of wealth in the former waste lands, and his own source of following in dependent broken men. The same developments occur in the Rajput lineage cycle in stage two, although a pre-existing external territorial state mixes into local proceedings. This social change is precisely what Lyall and Wills identified as the growth of feudalism out of the tribal heritage and convinced them that a kin-based society was not analogous to a feudal or state-based society. For, after all, the structure of the one excluded the other.

Perhaps Maine had these writers in mind when he wrote:

It has been not uncommon . . . sharply to contrast Celtic tribal customs with feudal rules, and doubtless between these customs and feudalism in its perfected state there are differences of the greatest importance. Yet if the testimony of the Brehon [Irish] tracts may be trusted, such differences arose, not from essential distinctions, but . . . from distinctions of degree in comparative social development. The germs of feudalism lay deep in the more ancient social forms. . . . This natural growth of feudalism was not, as some eminent recent writers have supposed, entirely distinct from the process by which the authority of the Chief or Lord over the Tribe or Village was extended, but rather formed part of it. While the unappropriated waste lands were falling into his domain, the villagers or tribesmen were coming through natural agencies under his personal power.[37]

From kinship to feudalism; such is the message of Maine's Irish material. We need not accept Maine's use of the term feudal to describe such social developments.

37. *Ibid.*, pp. 167–168.

What happens in Ireland is the growth of a centralized state wherein chiefly power emanates from sources outside the kin sphere. This social development does not prevent the previous kin-based polity from being regarded as a state or feudal-like—only that a new order has been introduced, in this instance by internal differentiation in terms of power and wealth of the chief from the mass of kin brethren.[38] What Lyall and Wills described as the evolution from tribal to feudal society is in reality the movement to a different form of state society, a closer approach to the ultimate territorial state structure freed from kin groups and familistic restraints. This evolution is not, however, a change from one quite distinctive social compact to another wholly different one. As Maine indicates, the kin structure and kin chief pave the way for the development of a "feudalistic," exploitative nonkin ruler.

The Irish and Chattisgarh histories chart the develop-

38. A recent book on political anthropology makes a distinction similar to my differentiation of kin-feudated states from territorial states. However, it differs both in name and concept from this presentation. Morton Fried in *The Evolution of Political Society* has distinguished "stratified" societies from "state" societies. The former are based on kin organization and do not have the constellation of political and judicial powers which define a state. Stratified societies are primarily characterized by an unequal access to strategic or subsistence goods so that economic classes come into existence, but have not yet polarized sufficiently for state political institutions to come into being.

Fried might argue that the Chattisgarh, Barabhum, and ancient Irish political orders should be termed stratified. Differentiation of such societies from centralized territorial states is clearly valuable. But Fried does more than that in his distinction between "stratified" and "state". He argues that economic differentiation into classes always precedes the formation of a state institutional fabric. The distinction between "stratified" and "state" is thus an invariable (purported) evolutionary process masquerading as a typological category. Because the following argument is predicated on a multicausal view of state formation, I do not follow Fried's classification.

ment of centralized state polity out of kin polity through internal differentiation. These examples prove the presence of kin organization in state societies and demonstrate the manner in which it forms the processural chain for future state developments which break out of the kinship mold. I now wish to turn to an analysis of developed territorial polities. Unlike kin-feudated states, territorial states depend on an organization of power and wealth inequality outside an all-encompassing kinship framework. Specialized institutions such as judicial systems, bureaucracies, standing armies, and territorial administration replace the cohesion supplied by a kin order. The following pages describe three societies known from archaeological research. They were all more politically sophisticated than Barabhum, Chattisgarh, or Ireland. They illustrate, however, the retention and effective use of kin machinery similar to Irish tribes or Bhumij clans within centralized political domains. The Aztec, Inca, and Mesopotamian states reproduce quite closely the pattern of external linkage between state and kin-defined locality of northern India. They also show the increasing abrogation of the local kinship order as the state grows stronger and more centralized.

TERRITORIAL STATES

The following presentation of Azetec, Inca, and Mesopotamian archaeological materials is hardly exhaustive. The data are meant to be suggestive and used for comparison; they do not claim to be definitive.

In present-day Andean society, an *ayllu* consists of several unrelated Indian families living together and practicing crop rotation under informal leaders.[39] In the

39. John H. Rowe, "Inca Culture at the Time of the Spanish Conquest," in *Handbook of South American Indians*, II, 253.

past, however, the ayllu was a kin-defined local social group which also had a part in the low-level administration of the Inca state. The absence of kin definition in the present ayllu is the result of the growth of a state bureaucratic fabric directly at odds with the maintenance of kin jurisdiction.

In traditional Andean society, the ayllu was an endogamous kinship group in which descent was traced through the male line and undoubtedly corresponded to what Sahlins has called a "ramage" and what Kirchhoff referred to as a "conical clan." [40] Each ayllu inhabited a definite territory and controlled certain agricultural lands. The extent of an ayllu's geographical spread and political dominance varied greatly in pre-Inca times. Around Cuzco, for example, independent ayllus were constantly contending for political domination. In other places, ayllus probably composed the local level of the native states and confederacies.[41]

The ayllu was the lowest level of state administration in the organization of the relatively late Inca empire. The Inca state was divided into four quarters which intersected at the royal capital of Cuzco. Each quarter was in turn divided into provinces. Below the provincial level was the "moiety." Generally two and sometimes three moieties existed in each province. Finally each moiety was composed of varying numbers of ayllus which differed in size. An ayllu was led by a hereditary leader whose status in the Inca administrative chain depended on the size of his ayllu.[42] The ayllu leader was confirmed in his hereditary office by accepting state authority.

40. For the concept of "ramage," see Marshall Sahlins, *Social Stratification in Polynesia,* p. xi; for the definition of "conical clan," see Paul Kirchhoff, "The Principles of Clanship in Human Society," in Morton H. Fried ed., *Readings in Anthropology,* II, pp. 259–270.

41. Rowe, *op. cit.,* p. 256.

42. *Ibid.,* p. 263.

The ayllu was a basic economic unit of Inca society. It provided labor, agricultural goods, and other services which supported the state elite and permitted the roads and monumental architecture with which the ruling class symbolized its power.[43]

Traditional political organization was radically altered after the Spanish conquest of the Inca empire. The ayllu has become a non-kin, cooperative village institution. Yet this development was foreshadowed in the state system of the Incas. Rowe notes:

> While most administrative Ayllus [under the Incas] were probably merely the old kin groups given an official place in the state structure, there is no doubt that the *Inca* regrouped the Ayllus and even created new ones when the native divisions were too small or otherwise not adapted to the purposes of *Inca* administration. The transformation of the Ayllu from a kinship group to a village group of independent families linked more by common residence than by descent already had a good start under the *Inca*.[44]

The Inca restructuring of the ayllu is reminiscent of the actions of a strong state in northern India during stage three of the developmental cycle. The ayllu itself is analogous to the Rajput stratified lineage, at least in so far as ayllus were absorbed into the administration of a centralized state. The Rajput lineage differed, however, in internal organization from the ayllu because it prescribed exogamy.

Aztec and Mesopotamian state forms also incorporated kinship groups at the local level. In his comparison of the political evolution of early Mesopotamia and prehispanic Mexico, Adams recognizes a general shift from ascriptively defined kinship groups to politically organized

43. *Ibid.,* p. 255.
44. *Ibid.,* p. 263.

units based on territory and residence.[45] He agrees with Kirchhoff, however, in recognizing that kin groups such as "conical clans" may have laid the basis for larger state developments.[46]

In Early Dynastic and Akkadian Mesopotamia, evidence of corporate, kin-based land-holding units has been discovered. Kin groups specializing in specific occupations also existed. Even when not directly noted, such kin bodies may have played important roles in many social institutions. The militias of Early Dynastic states were composed of platoons of craftsmen and other specialists led by their regular foremen. These platoons formed military companies under the direct control of a palace functionary. Adams suggests that such administratively defined foremen may have been in reality the ascriptively defined headmen of their kin-occupational groups.[47]

As in pre-Columbian Peru, the later history of Mesopotamia shows an erosion of the functions of such kin bodies as they are gradually replaced by centralized state administrative machinery or nonkin institutions. Even in early dynastic times, evidence indicates that private land holdings outside of a kin corporation existed which Adams believes indicates the initial decay of kin institutions.[48]

Data from pre-Columbian Aztec Mexico are more extensive. The Aztec kin body which was incorporated into low-level state administration is called the *calpulli*. Adams writes,

While debate continues over the precise nature of the calpullis, the trend of all more recent research supports the

45. Robert McC. Adams, *The Evolution of Urban Society. Early Mesopotamia and Prehispanic Mexico*, p. 80.
46. *Ibid.*, p. 93.
47. *Ibid.*, pp. 85–86.
48. *Ibid.*, p. 83.

conclusion that they were localized endogamous lineages that under most circumstances maintained their own lands and temples and that, particularly in urbanized, politically organized communities, also exercised a variety of functions.[49]

The corporately owned calpulli lands provided both house plots and cultivated fields for its members. If a field fell out of cultivation due to the demise of a family or a change of residence, the calpulli officers reapportioned the lands or had fields worked corporately to meet state tribute payments.[50] Equality of wealth or redistribution of land was not, however, the norm within a calpulli. Great variations grew up over time in the amount of land held by individual calpulli families. Some calpulli members were landless—whether by birth or individual misfortune is unclear. Such underprivileged individuals were forced into slavery or outmigration.[51]

Calpulli officers were chosen in much the same fashion as the chiefs of Irish tribes. They were the elected representatives of the entire kin body, but were generally drawn from a single, senior descent line within the calpulli. These officers were the intermediaries between the local calpulli and national state. The same lack of intrusion into local affairs which characterized the North Indian state in its relations with early stages of the Rajput cycle held true for the early Aztec state:

The need for central accounting was at a minimum under the system, and the apparatus of direct state control did not extend further into the body politic than the traditional leaders or representatives of the local community . . . the latter . . . continued to be defined on the bases not only

49. *Ibid.*, p. 87.
50. *Ibid.*, p. 88.
51. *Ibid.*

of localized residence and corporate control of land but also of real or fictive kinship. [52]

Originally, the Aztec state depended on the surplus production of the calpullis. "Internal tribute" was organized around the cultivation of fields expressly set aside for the state within a calpulli territory. Urban calpullis manufactured extra craft items for state use. During the period of great expansion of the Aztec state in the fifteenth century, calpullis became increasingly valued for their military role. These kin bodies served as corporate military units with their own emblems and leadership.[53]

The external sources of wealth and power which accrued to the Aztec state through conquest radically altered the kin fabric of the society. Wolf describes the political elite of the Aztecs before 1430 as consisting of a hereditary nobility who claimed a different descent from the mass of the population, but who probably derived from descendants of calpulli leaders.[54] The Aztec elite practiced status endogamy and enjoyed various social prerogatives "without at the same time possessing a source of economic power that could render them independent of the commoners, organized in their calpulli. The nobles were entitled to receive tribute from the calpulli, but had no access to land as such." [55] After 1430, the Aztecs defeated the Tepanecs, and the nobles gained an external source of land and labor. Wolf comments:

The strategic booty of the Tepanec war was land in the conquered provinces—land and peasants tied to the land. This land was used to underwrite the privileges of a warrior elite independent of popular jurisdiction.[56]

52. *Ibid.*, p. 91.
53. *Ibid.*, p. 89.
54. Eric R. Wolf, *Sons of the Shaking Earth*, pp. 136–137.
55. *Ibid.*, p. 137.
56. *Ibid.*, p. 139.

Wolf also notes that the Aztec rulers settled their own laborers on these lands. The new population consisted of broken men fleeing from other towns and districts and men standing outside the calpulli system. Such persons became just as dependent and shackled to the nobles as their equivalents in medieval Ireland. The wealth flowing in from tributary areas also permitted Aztec nobles "to create a nobility of service as well as a nobility of lineage, by rewarding . . . commoners who had distinguished themselves in warfare or in trade." [57]

As the Aztecs prospered, central authority redefined and encroached upon the autonomy and solidarity of the calpullis. External tribute beyond the requirements of the Aztec state was redistributed to the population in calpullis. The state gave rewards of land and goods to its calpulli militias. Central authority subsidized the poor and assumed the expenses of many festivals. Adams speculates that internal stratification within the calpulli increased, and the greater emphasis on the military stance brought about new leadership requirements.

The calpulli—like the Inca ayllu and the Mesopotamian kin bodies—increasingly gave up its kin structure in favor of the territorial arrangements of the state. Adams concludes:

Thus the sharp division between political patterns of organization at the upper levels and solidary kin communities comprising the great bulk of the population at the lower levels must have tended to blur and disappear more or less rapidly during the final decades of Aztec rule.[58]

Adams does introduce a caveat. The "politicization" of the calpulli was most advanced in urban areas. Even then, the primary loyalties of the majority of the Aztec

57. *Ibid.*
58. Adams, *op. cit.*, p. 90.

population were to such kin and residential groups. The calpulli perhaps continued as a significant kinship unit in terms of general social organization and local ideology; but it seemingly ceased to operate as an effective organizational element in the state, at least in the guise of a kin-defined body.

The analysis of territorial states has indicated that in other contexts outside of medieval India, kinship groups played important roles in the administrative apparatus of the state. Perhaps if more information were available on the calpulli and ayllu, we should find that they too underwent a developmental cycle. However, as these institutions are portrayed in the literature, they are half-way houses on the road from kin-based polity to the territorial state. Yet they do not appear solely as familistic impediments to the evolutionary process. Their role in the development of the territorial state is dramatic: in the early period they provide military contingents, craft goods, general subsistence, and, undoubtedly, sumptuary privileges to their high-ranking leaders, the future elites of the centralized political domain. Similarly, in India, it is not just by chance or cultural atavism or social redundancy that the Rajput stratified lineage is engrafted into state governmental procedures. Such lineages were in most periods the only successful and dependable means by which royal courts could insure the collection of revenue from local communities and could hope to maintain a minimum of law and order.

SUPERSTRATIFICATION AND THE STATE

What do Inca ayllus, Aztec calpullis, Rajput lineages, Bhumij clans, Chattisgarh rajadoms, and Irish tribes tell us about the origin and formation of the state? This problem has intrigued professional and amateur commentators over a long period. The answers vary greatly: some theorize that the state arises through social compact, others argue by conquest, and still others say as guarantor of the privileged against the poor.[59] Fried has recently contributed an original analysis and summary of the matter. In his discussion of the rise of the state, he restricts his definition of state to what I have called the "territorial state." [60] He has made an important distinction between those states which were pristine and those which were secondary in origins. The latter owe their rise to direct or indirect social stimulus from the pre-existant pristine states. Fried argues that the conditions which led to the rise of secondary states may not be important diagnostics for the growth of pristine states. Conversely, the conditions which promoted original states may no longer obtain in the secondary state development. Fried forcefully rejects conquest as the cause of the pristine state. He argues that conquest only leads to the "superstratification" of societies in already existant states. Rather than catapulting a society into statehood, conquest only reinforces a pre-existant stratification by providing more wealth, labor and territory to the state's rulers. Fried suggests that demographic imbalances may be clues to the origins of pristine states. Land scarcity in one kin segment of a tribal society coupled with land surplus in another might cause a demographic shuffle and create disenfranchised populations within kin-based communities.[61]

In Fried's terms, only the Aztec, Inca, and Mesopo-

59. For a review of these theories, see Lawrence Krader, *Formation of the State,* especially p. 44.

60. See note 38 of this chapter.

61. Fried, *The Evolution of Political Society,* pp. 19–226. The term, "superstratification," is used by Fried, "On the Evolution of Social Stratification and the State," *Culture in History: Essays in Honor of Paul Radin,* p. 729.

tamian states represent pristine developments. Barabhum, Ireland, Chattisgarh, and northern India are secondary states. Yet significant similarities exist between some pristine and secondary states which may belie Fried's analysis. These similarities are discussed below. The analytic framework of the discussion is derived from Fried's concept of "superstratification," although with some major redefinition. I should like to define "superstratification" as the process by which ruling elements emerge from a kin-feudated state rather than as a result of conquest. Such elements rip through the genealogical cover which had tied their political activities to the expansive familism of the group. Spurious pedigrees are invented which align elites with the sun or the moon or far-off royal houses, rather than the genealogy which places them only slightly senior to their commoner-kinsmen. When a society becomes superstratified, a class of rulers emerges whose allegiances are to themselves, their power, and their wealth. In the transition from a kin-based polity to a territorial political domain, we have seen that local-level kin groups are an important and even indispensible part of the developmental process. But at some point they become outmoded and decadent. Local kin groups attempt to confine exploitation and suppression by the state power within the boundaries defined by kin etiquette, albeit distant. If the polity is to emerge in a territorial form, superstratification must take place—a class must be broken free of kin restraints.

The foregoing materials have shown that such developments have often occurred both in pristine and secondary states. This is the process that Wills and Lyall refer to as the movement from tribalism to feudalism. It occurred in the Chattisgarh highland states and among the Irish tribes; it took place among the Incas and on the central Mexican plateau. I have not supplied a directly equivalent picture (in terms of process) for the Rajput lineage of northern India. Nevertheless, various stages in the developmental cycle are analogous. I have discussed, for instance, the process by which the state attempts to set aside the lineage elite and penetrate directly local kin groupings.

The various instances of superstratification illustrate the ways in which the centralized, nonkin, territorial state is born. In Chattisgarh and Ireland internal "colonization" of the kin body results in superstratification. The chief rescinds the kin polity, develops new outside sources of wealth by importing broken men or immigrants who owe allegiance directly to him. From these beginnings the autocratic and exploitative powers of the once-tribal chief, now turned "feudal" despot, develop. A similar evolution, in miniature, takes place in stage two of the Rajput cycle. The lineage raja collects his lowly kinsmen whose patrimony is not sufficient to support themselves and who must turn to service with the elite for subsistence. The evolution of such superstratification through internal colonization of the kin body fits Fried's demographic model for the pristine state. Inequalities in access to land and other "basic resources" lead to social differentiation within the kin group and nullify kin principles in favor of those based on power and wealth.

Superstratification may also arise from external colonization and conquest. The Aztec material reflects this evolution. External sources of wealth, power, and labor accrued to the Aztec nobility as a result of their military conquests and freed the elite from dependency on the calpulli. The calpulli was greatly transformed by the growing economic and political power of the elite. Again, similarities to the Rajput developmental cycle are evident. Conquest of weak neighboring stratified lineages occurs in stage two and the lineage raja uses these foreign territories and peoples as sources of political and economic advantage over his kinsmen. He attempts to strip his brethren of their proprietary rights and acts to reduce them to the status of tenants. Here, as in the case of internal colonization of the Rajput lineage, the existence of a higher level of central authority sets limits on local developments which did not enter into the Irish or Aztec situation. For instance, if the state is strong, it may effectively shield a lineage population from the exploitation of its raja by setting him aside, or by promoting fear of state retaliation to the point where he is unwilling to alienate his lineage military forces. Conversely, if the lineage raja has been successful in seizing the rights of his lineage mates, the state will often coopt him into its administrative apparatus and courtly life. In becoming a courtier and state appointee, the raja ceases to be an independent local figure, and can only exercise power over his lineage as a court favorite or state official. Although differing from either the Aztec or the Irish, the Rajput development nevertheless indicates a shared dynamic structure in territorial state formation which transcends region, culture, or conditions of inception.

The discussion above departs from Fried's demographic thesis of the rise of pristine states. The discussion also questions, at least sometimes, the distinction between pristine and secondary state origin. Both external conquest and internal colonization produce wealth and power inequalities leading to superstratification within a kinfeudated regime.

The focus of this chapter has been a comparison of the Rajput data from northern India with data from other areas. What bound the peoples of Chattisgarh, Ireland, Barabhum, Mexico, Incaland, and Mesopotamia together was the important role of corporate kinship groups in the organization of polity. I have examined both the correspondence between the internal order of the Rajput stratified lineage and various kin-feudated states, and the similarity in the encapsulation of kin-based divisions within the low-level administrative framework of centralized territorial states. These state forms directly contradict some cherished notions of political anthropology, especially belief in the incongruity of kin corporateness and territorial statehood. As a statement of structural opposition at either extreme, the notion may still be valid, but as an explanation of the developmental process of centralized polities, it is wanting. In its early stages, the territorial state depends on kin-based economic, military, and political groups.

This chapter has also tried to dipose of another anthropological chestnut—the conception, based on shopworn evolutionism, that the kin-based polities of India were by definition tribal and not state-level or feudal. In Barabhum, Rajasthan, Chattisgarh, and among the Rajput lineages of northern India, kinship did indeed organize internally differentiated and stratified bodies. What various scholars identified as the development of Indian familistic or tribal society into feudalism was actually the growth of superstratification and the movement towards a territorial, centralized state. Such superstratification necessarily destroys the kin bodies which presaged its own growth. I have suggested in this chapter that superstratification emerges through status and power inequalities within a society, either through external colonization and conquest or through internal disenfranchisement and vassalage. Once we understand that the major breakthrough in the evolution of a nonkin territorial state is the creation of suprakin identities, then a simple explanation of state origin (such as conquest or internal demographic imbalance) loses its appeal. Why a particular state developed must be investigated within the context of local ecology, demography, and culture contact. However, the process and changing structure of state development is constant: the nullification of kin groups under the superior stratification of an elite ruling class.

One major problem remains. In Mesopotamia, the Andean region, and Mexico, superstratification occurred —and the ayllu, calpulli and stratified kin groups gave way to the administration of the centralized territorial state. This final resolution does not seem to occur for the Rajput stratified lineages of northern India. Rather, a reoccurring cycle of state control followed a revitalization of local kin groups. No unilineal evolutionary path leads from kin-tribal to state-territorial organization. Until the British completely vitiate the traditional system, kin groups—stratified lineages—remain important adjuncts of local state government. Are we yet again faced with India, Unique and Oriental? The following chapter entertains this problem.

5

CONCLUSION: COMMUNITY AND STATE IN NORTHERN INDIA

T H E R O L E of genealogical reckoning in local-level political activity in northern India has been the major focus of this essay. In an attributional sense having to do with the duplication of patterns and principles of organization rather than direct behavioral involvement, kinship cemented local with regional and national levels of society. The various strata of agnatic descent—from minimal lineage to clan of identification—share a common social phraseology, whether solely for genealogical reasons or for status-political reasons. A local minimal lineage wishing to establish its identity as the preeminent line within a stratified lineage uses the same kin symbolism as the caste category or subregional varna.

The Rajput developmental cycle identifies another linkage between community and nation, namely the specific political and economic duties delegated from the central authority to the local level. Kinship organized local political groups such as the stratified lineage and its elite. Both state and stratified lineage are entwined in a relationship of distrust and exploitation, characterized by threat and counterthreat, and enforced by violence or revolt. Although neither party recognizes the other, their fortunes are inextricably bound up, so that changes at the state level precipitate local changes and vice versa. The lineage raja and elite are at the same time players and pawns. Their intermediary role between state and kin-defined locality sometimes brings affluence and power, at others disinheritance and deposition, or even rustication and banditry.

Five stages characterize the developmental cycle of the Rajput stratified lineage in northern India. During each stage the relationship of locality and state (intermediated by the lineage elite) altered radically. At times the state was strong and imposed its administrative organization directly on village communities, setting lineage raja aside, depriving village zamindars of many proprietary rights, and reducing the kin body to an egalitarian, fragmented, and relatively powerless political institution. In such periods, the state directly intervenes. It limits lineage migration and conquest, and cuts down the man-made jungles in which the dispossessed lineage elite take cover. In times of state weakness, other patterns of political mutualities regulate state-locality interaction. State anarchy or local impotence call forth lineage founders who stake claims to autonomy as they carve out kin-defined principalities. Their descendants may prevail over the kin brethren and assert their preeminence as lineage rajas empowered with state revenue duties and management over lineage conquests. The raja may continue to grow at the expense of his lineage mates until he expands beyond the kin realm and is coopted by the royal court, or in his own right, becomes potentate to his socially discarded distant kinsmen whom he now rackrents and disjoins. The developmental cycle approach allows a view of the great variety of social arrangements permissible within a single institutional framework. It avoids many of the problems which the British authorities created for themselves in the revenue management of northern India. The developmental cycle analysis does not prove that local revenue intermediaries were in some cases merely court favorites and in others, hereditary lineage leaders, as some British officials believed. It does not argue that severalty village organization takes historical precedence over the joint form, or that bhaiacharya and pattidari land tenures stand in an invariable causal sequence. No such easy theory of single-stranded evolution can characterize the complexity of tenurial and political organization in the hinterlands of the North Indian state. The economic and political chain between central authority and stratified lineage is many-linked, just as the multiple levels of corporate kinship behavior or genealogical identification are dizzying.

State-hinterland relationship in Rajput northern India has two aspects: ideological and attributional continuity depends on kinship which links the local lineage with the dispersed caste category and with the subregional varna; interactional integration consists of cyclic patterns of political behavior between localized stratified lineages and central authority. The continuity between the interactional and attributional linkages of local kin community and region or state is in the social form on which they depend. Whether manifested by claims to genealogical status as Chauhan or Rajput, or by direct behavioral display such as a raja calling forth his kin militia, unilineal kin groups and unilineal kin reckoning are the major constituents of state-hinterland interaction. We may define

India in many ways. However, a definition which departs too much from the organizational and ideological framework of unilineal kinship will discount the importance of caste, varna, pargana, and state in their traditional context.[1] Analysis of kin-feudated and territorial state societies in several world regions aids our understanding of Indian organization and indicates that India is not unique in its kin-locality linkage. Encapsulation of corporate kin bodies within state administrative apparatus characterized other societies. Even the internal order of Rajput stratified lineages can be matched in tribal populations in India and ancient societies of Europe.

Is India, then, only a variant of the Aztec and Inca structure? Not quite, for the problem posed at the end of the last chapter still remains: Why did kin organization at the local level in India not give way to superstratification and the growth of a territorial state? Why was political evolution in this direction circumvented when it occurred? Why was the territorial state merely a passing stage in the Rajput developmental cycle? The question phrased in this way asks for a causal recipe of Indian historical development, the nature of the ingredients, and how they combined. Such a request goes too far, at least for this study. A little speculation, however, is tempting. All writers who have viewed caste in India as a distinctly Indian phenomenon (even though some of them allowed aspects of it could be found in other societies and times) precede me in this. Such a drone of scholarly voices can hardly be ignored, even if in all the din of research, a sufficient explanation of caste in India has not yet been provided. I look back now to the first chapter of this essay in which I quoted the somewhat obtuse comments of

1. Other studies have emphasized this point in rather different ways. See, for example, Nur Yalman, *Under the Bo Tree;* E. R. Leach, *Pul Eliya: Village in Ceylon.*

Leach and Redfield. They are strong spokesmen for the uniqueness of Indian caste and kinship. Such phrases as "caste indissolubly linked to pan-Indian civilization" or the even more telling statement of scholarly insight, "India is the picture of a tribal society rearranged to fit a civilization," inform us of something which several generations of researchers have deemed vital about India. Unfortunately their sentiments have too often been phrased in the cryptic language used by Redfield and Leach. We have analyzed the Rajput stratified lineage, the caste, and the subregional varna; we have compared India at length with states elsewhere. How do we apply our analysis to recognize the uniqueness of India perceived by so many scholars?

Again, the answer lies in the nature of kinship and genealogical reckoning in northern India. It is not a causal answer. I will try below to merely list certain associations of kin institutions with state forms that may define India's special quality. It is not even a very full answer. I limit myself to Rajput northern India, but even within this ill-defined region, many sections may not fit my interpretation. For these reasons it may not be a satisfactory answer. I pursue this discussion here because it may prove informative or illuminating to my colleagues, and because it gives me an oportunity to rationalize my own sense of India's uniqueness.

The problem, then, is why in northern India the territorial state does not prove preeminent over local kin-defined political and economic bodies. I suggest that the web of attributional genealogical linkage which bound local community to region may circumvent such a development. An additional factor is the heavy emphasis on exogamous, extensive (noncousin) marriage in northern India, which dispersed kin connections over wide areas. When a powerful state trounced the raja, reduced the village zamindars to cultivators, and disposed of the lineage as an effective political institution, some residual kin elements remained. For the most part, they were not behavioral elements and did not directly channel local economic and political behavior. An efficient state could drain all such corporate behavior from a local area and former kin body. The residual elements were the ideological commitment to the Rajwar, Chauhan or Rajput model—all of which were genealogically defined and which, in hard times, could reinforce the behavioral aspects of kinship. In the absence of the behavioral reality of the stratified lineage, the attributional linkage of geographically dispersed kin groups gave the concept of genealogical corporateness viability. On the individual level, this meant a continued belief in the worth of claiming to be a Rajkumar, Chauhan, or Rajput, even though at the local level state suppression of kin groups meant that such statuses were behaviorally worthless. At a regional level, such residual kin elements reinforced belief in the complex kin-based superstructure of the lineage of recognition and clan of identification—in other words, of caste and subregional varna. For now we come to the "structural" crux of the matter. Identities in terms of caste, subregional varna, and thus genealogical reckoning were not threatened by the behavioral sabotage of the kin system by the state if the attributional framework remained. The continued ideological identification at regional levels could never be effaced by the state in traditional northern India. Even the powerful British colonial government as well as the less effective government of independent India could not completely rid local groups of commitments to the old genealogical categories, although they have increasingly less behavioral importance today.

An important factor maintaining this regional (genealogical) symbolism is the North Indian marriage pattern.

Rowe, Gould, Srinivas, and others have noted the territorial extensiveness of North Indian marriage patterns, at least in comparison to many preindustrial agrarian societies.[2] Neither the Inca ayllu nor the Aztec calpulli followed the exogamous pattern of a Rajput stratified lineage or the even higher levels of the lineage of recognition. The definition given by Sahlins for the ramage and by Kirchhoff for a conical clan specifies some amount of (status) endogamy. In northern India the equivalent to the status endogamy of the ramage is the chain of hypergamy which regulates Rajput marriages, and the ideological convention which supposes that Rajput marriages in a westerly direction rank higher than those directed towards the east. In the ayllu and calpulli, status endogamy reinforced rank prerogatives and inequalities. In northern India, the equivalent Rajput function is handled within a regional network of hypergamy, which links dispersed and often socially disparate groups within a generalized marital exchange pattern. Throughout northern India, wife-givers rank lower than wife-takers, and this ideology of kin alliance becomes a behavioral embodiment of the principle of extensive marriage among the Rajputs. Leach's study of the Kachin and their institution of hypogamy describes the *mayu-dama* marital exchanges which similarly link widespread groups in a formal and ranked social relationship. Redfield's insight into the tribal qualities of India civilization appears increasingly relevant. Even after numerous state developments, the

2. Srinivas contrasts the "extensive" marriage pattern of northern India with the intensive form of southern India. See M. N. Srinivas, *Caste in Modern India and Other Essays*, p. 58. On North Indian marriage, see William L. Rowe, "The Marriage Network and Structural Change in a North Indian Community," *Southwestern Journal of Anthropology*, XVI (1960), 299–311 *passim;* Harold A. Gould, "The Micro-Demography of Marriages in a North Indian Area," *Southwestern Journal of Anthropology*, XVI (1960), 476–491 *passim.*

tribal bases of polities remained as an integral aspect of the political order. Rajput kinship in northern India is not reduced to family and household, but rather maintains its web-like quality, and its character as a widely-cast net subsuming many different territories and peoples. Just as no other complex society has developed caste structure so deeply as India, no other state society has maintained kin corporateness and genealogical attribution so widely.

Is this ideology of extensive kinship, this practice of status hypergamy over regions an impediment to the rise of a permanent territorial state in northern India? I have not argued this, for the question of causality is both strategic and, unfortunately, moot. I merely note that when the state is strong and locally intrusive, the kin behavioral order may be completely deposed and yet the attributional kin categories binding locality and region and regulating marriage remain. When the state weakens, such attributional survivals may provide the rationale and charter for a new growth of local corporate kin groups. Genealogical categories are like phosphorized halloween costumes. The sun may set on the interactional political fortunes of local corporate kin bodies, but the largely attributional categories of lineage, clan, caste, and varna would continue to glow eerily as luminiscent reminders of what once had been.

The structure of Rajput political interaction in northern India has hardly proved unique, although in comparison with other world areas some interesting notions about state formation have emerged. In the organization of ideological motifs and of the regulation of marriage, however, Rajput northern India is distant from other territorial state societies. Its compeers would seem to lie in the tribal world, as Redfield noted and as many believers in the uniqueness of Indian caste and kinship perhaps unconsciously suggest. We are, perhaps, not surprised to find that North Indian ideological motifs are distinctive, while structural institutions are comparable. Yet in the crucial question of state formation, these ideological motifs help define local kin-based structural institutions. The cross-cultural comparability of Indian social structure some-times grades smoothly into a pan-Indian uniqueness of ideological content. Which is, if one believes in the concept of culture, to be expected.

Local communities defined, and were defined by, the interactional and attributional aspects of Rajput kinship. In the former, they were often locked into state admin-istration as revenue sources and potential political power bases. Their presence, in turn, at the lowest rung of the state order conditioned the nature of political interaction between state and locality, and the very quality of North Indian state form. Similarly, the local community gen-erated many of the genealogical allegiances, status de-mands, and hypergamous marriage patterns incorporated into the kinship web of the Rajputs. In both interactional and attributional matters, the constituents of the local Rajput community—kinship and its derivative, caste—conditioned the state order and bound the region. At times the state prevailed, the local community endured, and the mutual ideology of locality and region was threat-ened. During other periods the state was weak, local Raj-put lineages autonomous, and the web of attributional genealogical reckoning spread to enmesh many commu-nities in the ideological model based on unilineal kinship.

The hypotheses in this study are highly speculative; the historical materials often scant. Yet the presentation, I hope, illustrates the widened viewpoint which anthropol-ogy can adopt if it embraces historical materials and looks beyond the local community to contemporary and past social behavior. Whether or not the developmental cycle of the Rajput lineage conforms in every detail to the scheme indicated above is not so important in the most general view. Rather, the ability to advance such notions illustrates the value of a supracommunity, historical viewpoint for the anthropology of complex societies. A chowder of community studies couched in the present is only a theoretical prelude to the richer, more complex dish that anthropology can serve.

BIBLIOGRAPHY

Adams, Robert McC. *The Evolution of Urban Society. Early Mesopotamia and Prehispanic Mexico.* Chicago: Aldine Press, 1966.

Anderson, Robert T. and Barbara Gallatin Anderson. *Bus Stop for Paris.* Garden City: Doubleday-Anchor, 1966.

Anonymous (M. P. Carnegy). "The Talookdaree Tenure of Upper India," *Calcutta Review,* XLIII (1866), 137–160.

Baden-Powell, B. H. *A Manual of the Land Revenue Systems and Land Tenures of British India.* Calcutta: Office of the Superintendent of Government Printing, 1882.

———. *Land Systems of British India,* 3 vols. London: Oxford University Press, 1892.

———. *The Indian Village Community.* London: Longmans, Green, 1896.

———. *Village Communities in India.* New York: Scribner's, 1899.

Bailey, F. G. *Politics and Social Change: Orissa in 1959.* Berkeley and Los Angeles: University of California Press, 1963.

———. "Closed Social Stratification in India," *Archives Europeannes de Sociologie,* IV (1963), 107–124.

Benett, W. C. *A Report on the Family History of the Chief Clans of the Roy Bareilly District.* Lucknow: Government Press, 1870.

———. *Report of the Final Settlement of the Gonda District.* Allahabad: Government Press, 1878.

Butts, H. H. *Report of the Land Revenue Settlement of the Lucknow District.* Lucknow: Government Press, 1873.

Cohn, Bernard. "Political Systems in Eighteenth Century India: The Benares Region," *Journal of the American Oriental Society*, LXXXIII (1962), 312–320.

————. Review of "Caste Ranking and Community Structure in Five Regions of India and Pakistan," *Journal of the American Oriental Society*, LXXXII (1962), 425–430.

————. "Structural Change in Indian Rural Society," *Land Control and Social Structure in Indian History*. Ed. by Robert Eric Frykenberg. Madison: University of Wisconsin Press, 1969, 53–122.

Coulborn, Rushton. "Feudalism, Brahmanism, and the Intrusion of Islam Upon Indian History," *Comparative Studies in Society and History*, X (1968), 357–374.

Crooke, W. *The Tribes and Castes of the North-Western Provinces and Oudh*. 4 vols. Calcutta: Office of Government Printing, 1896.

Currie, Robert G. *Report on the Settlement of the Shahjehanpore District*. Allahabad: Government Press, 1874.

Dumont, Louis. *Hierarchy and Marriage Alliance in South Indian Kinship*. London: Occasional Papers of the Royal Anthropological Institute of Great Britain and Ireland no. 12, 1957.

Duthoit, W. "On Ryot Right in the Family Domains of the Raja of Benares," in W. Muir, *Notes on Tenant Right, On Rights to Subsettlement, and on Rights of Jagheerdars*, Allahabad: Government Press, 1869.

Elliot, H. M. *Memoirs on the History, Folk-lore, and Distribution of the Races of the N.W.P., Being an Amplified Edition of the Original Supplemental Glossary of Indian Terms by the Late Sir H. M. Elliot*. Ed. and revised by J. Beames. London: J. Trubner, 1869.

Elliott, Charles Alfred. *Chronicles of Oonao*. Allahabad: Allahabad Mission Press, 1862.

Forbes, W. E. *Report on the Revenue Settlement of the Partabgarh District*. Lucknow: Government Press, 1877.

Fortes, Meyer and E. E. Evans-Pritchard. *African Political Systems*. London: Oxford University Press, 1941.

Fox, Richard G. "The British Settlement of the North-

Western Provinces, 1801–1822." (Unpublished manuscript, 1962.)

———. "Varna Schemes and Ideological Integration in Indian Society," *Comparative Studies in Society and History*, XI (1969), 27–45.

———. "Rajput 'Clans' and Rurban Centers in Northern India," *Urban India: Society, Space, and Image*. Ed. by Richard G. Fox (in press).

Freedman, Maurice. "A Chinese Phase in Social Anthropology," *British Journal of Sociology*, XIV (1963), 1–19.

Fried, Morton H. "The Classification of Corporate Unilineal Descent Groups," *Journal of the Royal Anthropological Institute of Great Britain and Ireland*, LXXXVII (1957), 1–29.

———. "On the Evolution of Social Stratification and the State," *Culture in History: Essays in Honor of Paul Radin*. Ed. by Stanley Diamond. New York: Columbia University Press, 1960, 713–731.

———. *The Evolution of Political Society*. New York: Random House, 1967.

Frykenberg, Robert Eric. "Traditional Processes of Power in South India: An Historical Analysis of Local Influence," *Indian Economic and Social History Review*, I (1963), 122–142.

Geertz, Clifford. *Agricultural Involution: The Process of Ecological Change in Indonesia*. Chicago: University of Chicago Press, 1963.

———. *The Social History of an Indonesian Town*. Cambridge: M.I.T. Press, 1965.

Goody, Jack ed. *The Developmental Cycle in Domestic Groups*. Cambridge: Cambridge University Press, 1958.

Gough, Kathleen and David Schneider, *Matrilineal Kinship*. Berkeley and Los Angeles: University of California Press, 1961.

Gould, Harold A. "The Micro-Demography of Marriages in a North Indian Area," *Southwestern Journal of Anthropology*, XVI (1960), 476–491.

Gupta, Sulekh Chandra. *Agrarian Relations and Early British Rule in India.* Bombay: Asia Publishing House, 1963.

Habib, Irfan. *The Agrarian System of Moghul India.* New York: Asia Publishing House, 1963.

Hasan, S. Nurul. "The Position of the Zamindars in the Moghul Empire." *Indian Economic and Social History Review,* I (1964), 107–109.

Hasan, S. Nurul. "Zamindars Under the Mughals," *Land Control and Social Structure in Indian History.* Ed. by Robert Eric Frykenberg. Madison: University of Wisconsin Press, 1969.

Hazlehurst, Leighton. "Multiple Status Hierarchies in Northern India," *Contributions to Indian Sociology,* New Series II (1968), 38–57.

Hutchinson, J. R. *Allyghur Statistics, Being a Report on the General Administration of that District from A.D. 1803 to the Present Time.* Roorkee: Thomason College Press, 1856.

Karve, Iravati. *Hindu Society: An Interpretation.* Poona: Deccan College Press, 1961.

Kaye, John William. *A History of the Sepoy War in India, 1857–58.* 3 vols. London: W. H. Allen, 1864–1876.

Kirchhoff, Paul. "The Principles of Clanship in Human Society," *Readings in Anthropology II.* Ed. by Morton H. Fried. New York: Crowell, 1959.

Krader, Lawrence. *Formation of the State.* Englewood Cliffs: Prentice-Hall, 1968.

Lattimore, Owen. "The Frontier in History," *Studies in Frontier History: Collected Papers, 1928–1958.* Oxford University Press and Paris: Mouton, 1962.

Leach, E. R. ed. *Aspects of Caste in South India, Ceylon, and Northwest Pakistan.* Cambridge: Cambridge University Press, 1960.

———. *Pul Eliya: Village in Ceylon.* Cambridge: Cambridge University Press, 1961.

Lenski, Gerhard. *Power and Privilege: A Theory of Social Stratification.* New York: McGraw-Hill, 1966.

Lloyd, Peter C. "The Political Structure of African Kingdoms: An Exploratory Model," *Political Systems and the Distribution of Power* (Association of Social Anthropologists monograph no. 2). New York: Frederick A. Praeger, 1965, 63–112.

Lyall, Alfred. *Asiatic Researches, Religious and Social.* London: John Murray, 1884.

Maine, Henry Sumner. *Village Communities in the East and West.* London: J. Murray, 1887.

———. *Lectures on the Early History of Institutions.* New York: Henry Holt, 1888.

Manners, Robert. "Remittances and the Unit of Analysis in Anthropological Research," *Southwestern Journal of Anthropology,* XXI (1965), 179–195.

Marriott, McKim. "Village Structure and the Punjab Government: A Restatement," *American Anthropologist* LV (1953), 137–143.

———. "Attributional and Interactional Theories of Caste Ranking," *Man In India,* XXXIX (1959), 106–121.

Mayer, Adrian C. Conference on New Approaches in Social Anthropology, Jesus College, Cambridge, England, 1963. "The Significance of Quasi-Groups in the Study of Complex Societies" in *The Social Anthropology of Complex Societies,* ed. by Michael Banton (Association of Social Anthropologists monograph, no. 4). London: Tavistock Publications, 1966; pp. 97–122.

Metcalf, Thomas. *The Aftermath of Revolt: India 1857–1860* Princeton: Princeton University Press, 1964.

———. "From Raja to Landlord: The Oudh Talukdars, 1850–1870," *Land Control and Social Structure in Indian History.* Ed. by Robert Eric Frykenberg. Madison: University of Wisconsin Press, 1969.

Millett, A. F. *Settlement of the Land Revenue of the Sultanpur District.* Lucknow: Government Press, 1873.

———. *Report of the Land Revenue Settlement of Fyzabad District.* Allahabad: Government Press, 1880.

Moreland, W. H. *The Agrarian System of Moslim India.* Delhi: Oriental Books, 1968 (1929).

Morgan, Lewis Henry. *Ancient Society*. Chicago: Charles Kerr, n.d.

Muir, W. *Notes on Tenant Right, On Right to Subsettlement, and On Rights of Jagheerdars*. Allahabad: Government Press, 1869.

Neale, Walter C. *Economic Change in Rural India: Land Tenure and Reform in Uttar Pradesh; 1800–1955*. New Haven: Yale University Press, 1962.

Neville, H. R. *Sultanpur: A Gazetteer*. United Provinces of Agra and Oudh District Gazetteers, Vol. XLVI. Allahabad: Government Press, 1908.

Oldham, Wilton. *Historical and Statistical Memoir of the Ghazeepoor District*. Allahabad: Government Press, 1870.

Orenstein, Henry. "Caste and the Concept, 'Mahratta,' in Maharasthra," *Eastern Anthropologist*, XVI (1963), 1–9.

Pocock, David, "Sociologies: Rural and Urban," *Contributions To Indian Sociology*, IV (1960), 63–81.

Pradhan, M. C. *The Political System of the Jats of Northern India*. Bombay: Oxford University Press, 1966.

Redfield, Robert. *Peasant Society and Culture*. Chicago: Phoenix Books, 1963.

———. "The Social Organization of Tradition," *Peasant Society: A Reader*. Ed. by May Diaz, Jack Potter, and George Foster. Boston: Little, Brown, 1967.

Roberts, D. T. *Report on the Revision of Records of Part of Ballia District*. Allahabad: Government Press, 1886.

Rowe, John Howland, "Inca Culture at the Time of the Spanish Conquest," *Handbook of South American Indians*, II: *The Andean Civilizations*. Ed. by Julian Steward (Bureau of American Ethnology Bulletin 143), 1946, 183–330.

Rowe, William L. "The Marriage Network and Structural Change in a North Indian Community," *Southwestern Journal of Anthropology*, XVI (1960), 299–311.

Rudolph, Suzanne. "The Princely States of Rajputana: Ethic, Authority, and Structure," *Indian Journal of Political Science*, XXIV (1963), 14–32.

Sahlins, Marshall. *Social Stratification in Polynesia*. Seattle: University of Washington Press, 1958.

Shah, A. M. "Political System in Eighteenth Century Gujarat," *Enquiry*, I (1964), 83–95.

Singh, K. N. "The Territorial Basis of Medieval Town and Village in Eastern Uttar Pradesh, India," *Annals of the Association of American Geographers*, LVIII (1968), 203–220.

Singh, R. L. and K. N. Singh. "Evolution of the Medieval Towns in the Saryu-par Plain of the Middle Ganga Valley: A Case Study," *The National Geographical Journal of India*, IX (1963), 1–11.

Sinha, Surajit. *State Formation and Rajput Myth in Tribal Central India*. Reprint no. 3, Program on Comparative Studies on Southern Asia of Duke University, n.d.

Skinner, G. William. "Marketing and Social Structure in Rural China, Part I," *Journal of Asian Studies*, XXIV (1964), 3–44.

Sleeman, W. H. *A Journey Through the Kingdom of Oude in 1849–1850*. 2 vols. London: Richard Bentley, 1858.

Smith, Marian W. "The Misal: A Structural Village-Group of India and Pakistan," *American Anthropologist*, LIV (1952), 41–56.

Southall, Aidan. *Alur Society*. Cambridge: W. Heffer, 1956.

———. "A Critique of the Typology of States and Political Systems," *Political Systems and the Distribution of Power*. Ed, by Michael Banton (Association of Social Anthropologists Monograph no. 2) New York: Frederick A. Praeger, 1965, 113–140.

Srinivas, M. N. *Caste in Modern India and Other Essays*. Bombay: Asia Publishing House, 1962.

Steward, Julian, *Area Research: Theory and Practice*. New York: Social Science Research Council, 1950.

Swartz, Marc J., Victor W. Turner, and Arthur Tuden eds. *Political Anthropology*. Chicago: Aldine, 1966.

Thomason, John. *Report of the Collector of Azimgurh on the Settlement of the Ceded Portion of the District Commonly Called Chuklah Azimgurh*. Agra: Government Press, 1837.

Thorner, Daniel. "Feudalism in India," *Feudalism in History*. Ed. by Rushton Coulborn. Princeton: Princeton Univeristy Press, 1956.

Thornton, John. "Report Upon the Settlement of Pergunnah Moorsan, Zilla Allyghur," reprinted in *Allyghur Statistics, Being a Report on the General Administration of that District from A.D. 1803 to the Present Time.* Roorkee: Thomason College Press, 1856.

Tod, James. *Annals and Antiquities of Rajasthan, or the Central and Western Rajput States of India.* Ed. by William Crooke. London: Oxford University Press, 1920.

Wheeler, P. C. *Revision of Records and Settlement Operations in Jaunpur District.* Allahabad: Government Press, 1886.

Wills, C. U. "The Territorial System of the Rajput Kingdoms of Medieval Chattisgarh," *Journal and Procedings of the Asiatic Society of Bengal,* New Series XV (1919), 197–262.

Wolf, Eric R. "Aspects of Group Relations in a Complex Society: Mexico," *American Anthropologist* LVIII (1956), 1065–1078.

———. *Sons of the Shaking Earth.* Chicago: University of Chicago Press, 1959.

Yalman, Nur. *Under the Bo Tree.* Berkeley and Los Angeles: University of California Press, 1967.

INDEX

Acephalous kin societies, 129-130
Adams, R. Mc., 152ff.
African political systems, 129ff.
Agnates, 36, 75; links to lineage elite, 70
Agra province, 62
Alla-ud-Din Ghori, 68
Andean society, 150ff.
Anderson, Robert and Barbara, 3
Attributional: definition of, 22n.12; categories, 34; life styles and models, 43, 44; linkage to larger society, 171
Attributional status, 43, 164, 166; and real vs. upstart Rajputs, 46; and subregional varna category, 43, 46; and territorial state, 168
Ayllu, 150, 151
Azamgarh district, 107
Aztec state, 153-157

Babus, 114
Bachgotis, 24-27, 30, 34, 35, 36, 37, 68, 85, 86, 107; composition of, 24, 25; dispersion of, 71
Bachgotis of Asal, 85
Baden-Powell, B. H., 18, 80, 98, 119, 121, 122; disagreement with H.S. Maine, 120, 122, 126-127
Bailey, F. G., 3, 9
Ballia district, 13, 18, 26, 27, 31, 36, 39, 51, 114
Balwant Singh (Raja of Banaras), 99, 116. See also Rajas of Banaras
Banaras region, 11. 13, 17, 24, 26, 27, 62, 114, 116
Bandits, 102-103
Barabhum, 137-140

Barriar Singh, 24, 107; as lineage founder, 68, 69
Basti district, 26
Benett, W. C., 39, 52, 73, 78, 79, 97, 98, 109, 112
Bengal, 54
Bhaiacharya land tenure, 61, 74, 113, 119-121; definition of, 59; development of from pattidari land tenure, 119, 122. See also bighadam land tenure, and Baden-Powell, B. H.
Bhars, 68
Bhuinhars, 17, 18, 22, 23
Bhumij state, 138-140, 141, 147
Bighadam land tenure, 121, 122
Blocks, 9
Brahman, 85
British revenue officers, 10, 117; assignment of proprietary rights by, 59; belief in tribal migration, 67; distinction between pattidari and bhaiacharya tenure by, 59; recognition of developmental cycle by, 61; recognition of new lineages by, 107, 108; recognition of political role of kin terminologies by, 26
Broken men, 146, 156
Butts, H. H., 111

Cadet kin lines, 32, 35, 36, 48, 51, 52, 71-73, 86; and grants from lineage elite, 95; problems posed by, 90, 91; provisions for, 70, 79; separation from raja of, 96, 97. See also Lineage elite
Calpulli, 153ff.

* 9 7 8 0 5 2 0 3 2 5 4 3 2 *